BEFORE THE INVENTION OF SMILING

The Incredible Journey of the Zucker Family from
Horse & Buggy to Indoor Plumbing

By David Zucker

Illustrations by
Cynthia Angulo

CONTENTS

Introduction...6

Part One: Hinkovitz 13

Part Two: America...70

Part Three: Burton..123

Part Four: David 166

Part Five: Charles & Sarah 195

INTRODUCTION

SUMERIAN COUPLE
1900 BC

RIFKA & ISAAC SRULOVITZ
1900 AD

Two couples.

On the left, an unknown Babylonian couple. On the right, my great grandparents. You'd think something would've changed in four thousand years, but... nothing. However, by the time their daughter, (my grandmother) Sarah was born, everything *did* change. Sarah and her siblings were about to enter the modern world, and begin a journey from no indoor plumbing, electricity, or telephones, to a world of automobiles, airplanes, moon landings, internet, computers, cellphones,— and her grandsons becoming Hollywood movie directors. This is the story of my family, including both the mundane and the bizarre. And it's all true. You couldn't make this stuff up.

INTRODUCTION

WHO CAME BEFORE GRANDPA? Me, age 4, with Dad, and Grandpa, who re-tied his necktie to match his son and grandson. Grandpa's straight face against his ridiculously oversized bow tie is pure Leslie Nielsen.

From the time I was just a little boy, growing up in Milwaukee, I was curious about the Zucker family, where we came from, our ancestry, etc. One day I asked my father:

"Dad, who came before Grandpa?"
"Grandpa Leo? Well, his father, Samuel Zucker."
"And who came before Samuel?"
"Um, Benjamin, I believe."
"And before him?
"Well, we don't know, exactly, but I suppose if you go back far enough, Moses."
"Gee. And who came before Moses?"
"Uh, Abraham."
"And who came before Abraham?"
"Well…Adam and Eve."
My eyes opened wide.
"Wow! You mean Adam and Eve were Zuckers!?"

This strange connecting of concepts in my brain synapses could well have lead to lines like *"And don't call me Shirley!"* and *"Nice Beaver!"* but apart from that, I've had a curiosity about history for as long as I can remember, perhaps inspired by the Davy Crockett craze of the mid 1950's.

INTRODUCTION

*FESS PARKER: As the famous frontiersman, at once a hero and my introduction to history. He called me 35 years later - with a script!

FESS PARKER FANS: Jerry and me, at the height of the Crockett craze, 1955. By age 17, he had made up the height difference.

It wasn't enough to shoot my toy rifle at imaginary bears while dressed in "buckskins" with plastic fringe and coonskin cap. I badgered my Dad with a million questions. "Could we see Davy's log cabin if we went to Tennessee?" "Is the Alamo still there in Texas?" "Where are all the real places he lived or traveled to?" "What's there now?" I wondered if maybe my own family could have had some small connection to real *history*.

Of course I was disappointed that the Zuckers had none, but growing up in Milwaukee, I remember listening to my grandmother, Sarah Zucker, spin tales of her life in late 19th century Hungary, in a little village called Hinkovitz. One of eight brothers and sisters, she was the only one who talked about it. And I was the only one of her ten grandchildren who listened (along with my cousin, Debbie Zucker) for hours at a time, fascinated by tales of her miraculous survival from a flash flood, the frustrating clash with her own mother who refused to leave Hungary, the escape in the dead of night through a forest across the border into Poland, and the arduous, sometimes dangerous journey by wagon, train and boat to a final destination in America. To me, this was the next best thing to being related to Davy Crockett.

Maybe the Zucker family had its share of high adventure after all.

1976: Back in Milwaukee with a tape recorder.

INTRODUCTION

Years later, after having moved to Los Angeles to create the Kentucky Fried Theater, I decided I'd better get Grandma's recollections recorded, concerned that if nothing was written down, all these stories would be lost. And if they had value for me, maybe in the future, my own children might be interested. So one day, in the Fall of 1976, on a visit to Milwaukee, Jerry and I sat down with Grandma, then 83, to get the whole story recorded.

We arrived at her apartment on Kensington Boulevard in Shorewood on a Saturday morning and got four hours on tape. Ten years later I had a transcript made, and there it sat, in a drawer, until 2003. By that time, I thought my own children, then aged 6 and 4, were ready to hear the story.

I decided to put it in a form they could understand, illustrating it with drawings where actual photographs weren't available. I recruited Gary Thomas, a storyboard artist I worked with on *The Naked Gun franchise*, and we created a "children's book" version, a somewhat fictionalized 3rd person narrative of the story. I didn't think it worked, and back in the drawer it went -- until about two years ago, when I happened to reread the transcript. But this time, it hit me that Sarah's true personality was revealed in her own words, as she was describing her feelings and opinions as well as events.

It was like having another visit on Kensington Blvd.

ILLUSTRATOR FORWARD

> On my first time meeting David, I realized how passionate he was about history, family, and the art of telling a story. Three things that I myself share a passion for. Whenever David told me a story about his family, he would inspire me to help tell his story in the only way I knew how - through drawing. And every conversation that we would have would result in some sort of history lesson, that would inform and enrich this book even more. As an artist, the challenge was to take all of this material and visualize it in a creative way. David had been collecting valuable family belongings, photographs, and documents for years. My job was to "fill in the gaps" of the story and recreate moments that weren't photographed. It was a long and detailed process of research, meetings (we would meet once a month at a Starbucks in El Segundo), notes, and revisions of drafts - but the attention to detail and storytelling was important for a project like this one. What's particularly unique about this book is that it is unlike any other: a documentary in book form, combining drawings with photographs. And thus, it has been an honor to be a part of this book and to be able to work with someone like David - who has told his story in order to inspire others to treasure their family history so that they may pass along their story as well. After all, aren't we a nation of storytellers ourselves?
> - Cynthia Angulo

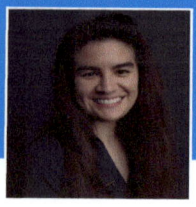

PART ONE

HINKOVITZ

This is the transcript of the recording I made in 1976 as we interviewed Grandma in her dining room. We brought with us maps to try to pinpoint the location of Sarah's hometown. Sarah's words appear in **BOLDFACE.**

David: Can you look at this and tell us where Hinkovitz was?
Sarah: Our town was in the Carpathian Mountains. On a road - it was called the Kaiser Strasse. The King's Highway. There were many little towns and villages on this road. It may be on there somewhere (indicates map) Between Dukla and…I forgot the name… But it's close to what you have there - not much, not as heavy as Dukla as at our place- and yet Dukla was north of us.

I get excited when I get to Palm Springs. I love mountains. Oh how I adored the mountains, yes, the Carpathian Mounbtains.

Have you been in Palm Springs?
Well, the valley was deeper than Palm Springs is, but surrounded by mountains like Palm Springs. Vegetation on those mountains, though. There were even cherry trees there.

EVERYTHING BUT CHERRY TREES: Sarah on a 1965 Palm Springs vacation with her younger brother, Uncle Maury.

Our village was right on the Kaiserstrasse. Other villages were away in the woods that you had to go look for; ours was right on the King's Highway. Komarnik was right on there.

FORMERLY AUSTRIA-HUNGARY: In 1976, "Czechoslovakia" The outlined area can be found in the map on the following page.

Do you remember something called Svidnik?
[Big reaction:] Oh! You don't say! Svidnik was walking distance from our house! That is South of us. That was very close! They had a 10 cent store in Svidnik. Boy, did I have a good time!

And that also was on the King's Highway?
Right, yes, on the same highway. Now we're getting somewhere!

How many villages were between Svidnik and Hinkovitz?
There was Lodomir, Charnow...

Could this be it? Hunkovce?
Let me see. Yes, that's it! It's in the right place. I just don't recognize that spelling.

A large town?
No. It was a village.

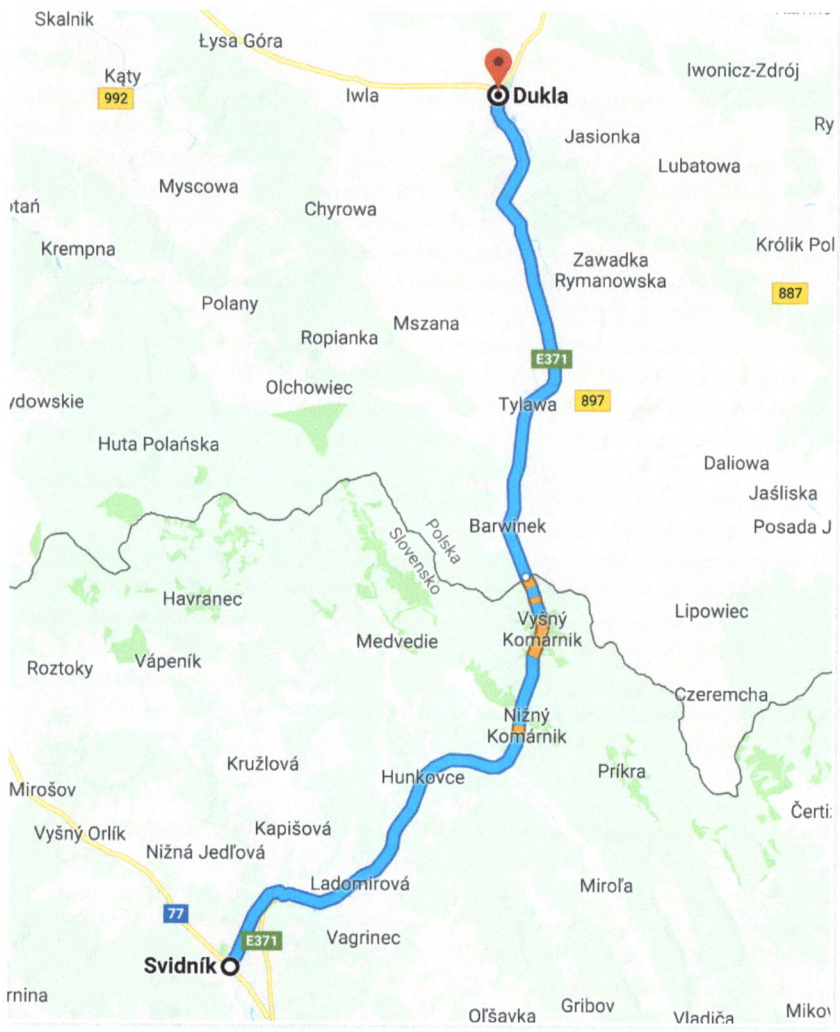

If we ever went back to Hinkovitz, is there a river or any landmarks that we could tell where your house was?

There's a river that goes right through the town. Not much of a river, just a very small … a little bit larger than a creek.

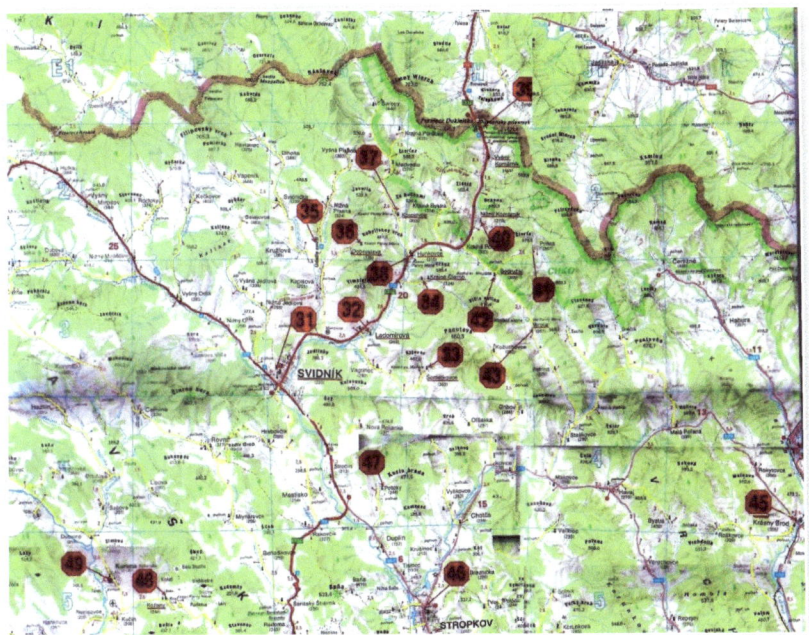

What was it called?
I have no idea. In Yiddish, "river" is *ya-dey*. But whether that was it, I don't know.

There was a bridge across it; the beams for the bridge were sent in from Milwaukee, from West Allis. The bridge was right in the town, practically in the middle of the town. It was just a little walking distance from us, not even a block at all.

Was that after it was destroyed in the flood?
Yes, that's right. When I was just a baby. I don't know how old exactly, but it had rained for days and days, maybe a whole week, and then one night there was a huge thunderstorm. My mother and father woke up in the middle of the night - to see water rushing into the house.

Father ran to get the other children, My mother, your great grandmother, Rifka, rushed out of the house with me. She was carried away by the water, trying to hold on to me. But just as we were about to go under, my Uncle Isador swam out and rescued me!

I met Nancy Stern Rosten, in Las Vegas in 2008 while I was there doing a panel. She introduced herself as a cousin. It turned out her father was Isador Stern, Rifka's youngest brother.

BEFORE THE INVENTION OF SMILING

> "At the time of the flood my father was 14. He told me that he saw your grandmother struggling in the water. So he dove in and managed to grab her, while the rest of the family waited on some higher ground, where it was still dry,
> near a church..
> - Nancy Stern Rosten"

> "You can imagine how relieved the family was to see my father appear, carrying your grandmother in his arms!
> - Nancy Stern Rosten"

When we finally got out of the water, Mother saw that I wasn't breathing! She was panicked, she thought I had drowned. But she put me to her breast and began to nurse me.

While this was all going on, there was a man who was sitting nearby, and he looks over at mother and says, "Lady, you got five other children, what does it matter if you lose this one?" Can you believe that? But then, suddenly, I started breathing again! — It's not such a surprise, (laughs) I'm here today!

But whenever Mother would tell me this story, and she told it many, many times, she would always say: "Remember, *Whoever saves one life, it is as if he saved the entire world.*" I think it's a quote from the Talmud.

MY IDEA OF A VACATION: After wrapping filming on Scary Movie 3, Anna Faris headed to Maui, Charlie Sheen, the beach at Ibiza. I went to Slovakia with Gary Thomas. We hired a guide and driver in Krakow, Poland, drove down the King's Highway, and found Hinkovitz!

OLDEST WOODEN CHURCH IN SLOVAKIA: I found the church, about two blocks from the river, and definitely on higher ground. Built in 1770, it was completely renovated in 2005-8 and houses very rare books from the 17th century. When I was there (2003) it was still under construction and closed.

How close was the church to your house?
We were very close, right near the bridge, the center of the village. Uncle Sam used to play with the Gypsy kids there. They taught him to play the violin.

Oh. Is that where Aunt Shirley got her interest in music?
You mean Shirley Brody? Oh yes! I suppose that is where!

DOCTORS SYMPHONY 1895: Sam Srulovitz with gypsy friends. Sam's daughter, Shirley became a violist and co-founder of the Los Angeles Doctors Symphony, in the 1950's, performing there with her husband, Dr. Jack Brody. [INSET] The Gypsies remain in the area to this day.

Did any of the other siblings have musical interest?
No, no. Aunt Frieda loved horses. She was a beautiful horse rider. She'd stand up straight on that horse . . . She was not scared of the wildest horse. She would climb up on top of it and fly away. She was really something, a daredevil. I guess she didn't realize how dangerous it was. And yet she never telephoned! And she never learned how to drive a car. That's something my mother never could get over. They tried. Jack (her husband) bought a car for her. She had lessons. But she didn't do it; she was scared.

BUT SHE COULD RIDE A HORSE: Frieda Srulovitz, Hunkovitz, c.1905

Is your house in Hinkovitz still there?
Dr. Ackerman who lived here in Milwaukee for many years, you've heard the name, he passed away recently - he had gone back to Europe several times because his parents lived in the same town we lived in, his parents were neighbors of ours. And each time he came back from Europe, he would call me up and tell me "Again, I'm reporting to you there isn't a sign of the place where your home was."

In September and October of 1944 the Russians fought the Germans in the Battle of Dukla Pass, at which time much of the village was destroyed. Even 60 years later there still remained rusted tanks, planes and artillery pieces.

But if I was to go back and try to find the location of the house, how would I find it? Now if this is the river, and this is the highway, the Kaiser Strasse…

Yes. Here's the Kaiser Strasse, which ran the long way in the valley. The villag was very long on one side and short and narrow on the other. This is the narrow end. And this would be West…

> *At this point, according to Grandma's descriptions, I began sketching a map.*

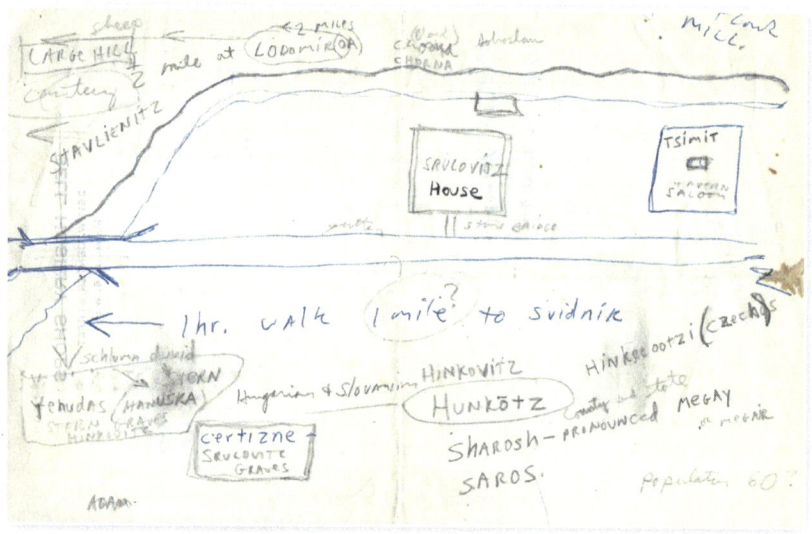

THE MAP: Other notes are scrawled on the margins. I took this with me on the 2003 trip.

And here's our house. Yeah. Our house is here. And the river is behind our house. And runs the same direction as the road.

Your house was between the river and the road?
Yes. Our house was on the road. Our porch was just a little bit off the road, so people could drive up [to the general store].

The river ran right near your backyard?
Yes. We had a barn in back, and adjoining the barn was the river. At that particular point, it was not much of a river.

HOUSE AND BARN: From the map (in my hand) drawn in Grandma's dining room, I was able to locate the spot where the Srulovitz house/store and barn likely stood. From the main road, the land sloped gently down to the river behind the barn, as Sarah described. Most likely, the current structures were built on the foundations of the original buildings.

How many houses were between your house and the bridge?
None.

SRULOVITZ PROPERTY: Our guide and translator, talking with the present owner in front of the rebuilt Srulovitz house.

Did Dr. Ackerman go back again?
Oh yes, he was there two or three times. On one of his trips he met his wife. He married a Budapest girl. She was 19 and now she must be close to 60. She has a son in San Francisco, a dentist, John Ackerman. She's a good friend of mine. We have a lot of fun when we get together. She knows that Jack knew me when I was a little girl. Jack and I were the same age.

Did you go to Budapest very often?
No, I was only in Budapest once. That was too far away from us, and transportation was bad. I made it because I had an aunt living near Botchkov - is that what you found there, Botchkov?

Something like that.

I was lucky. People would take a liking to me, relatives or someone, and they would invite me to come and visit with them. So I was lucky enough to get around to see those cities. And the cities were beautiful.

COPIES OF CASTLES: 1891, Schuster Mansion, Lake Drive, Milwaukee.

They had beautiful architecture, that's where I got so spoiled. I saw a lot of beautiful architecture. And then I came to Milwaukee and … oh boy. What they had.

I was a little bit lonely when I first came to Milwaukee. I promised myself I would go back. And when I met this guy Leo Zucker, and told him how I miss Europe and what a beautiful childhood I had, he said, "Well, as soon as I can pull things together, I'll take you to Europe. And I too want to go to Europe, to my mother's grave." He was only 12 years old when his mother died. He always said he would like to go back to Europe to put a monument on her grave. Well, we never did. Oh, I looked forward to going back to Hinkovitz, but I got along without it.

What was the reason you left in the first place?
The army needed soldiers. Mother didn't want my brothers going into the army, because they would have to eat *treif*. (Non kosher food) We always had trouble with the Poles and with the Russians. Sometimes we'd see them passing on the road.

Soldiers?
Right. And we'd be frightened stiff. You'd think there'd be war the next day. And the Jews were hit first.

SARAH'S MEMORY: Hungarian soldiers marching through Hinkovitz.

Did you hear stories of pogroms in the other towns?
Listened to it day and night, the pogroms, in Russia.

But your town really didn't…
No. No. We lived at peace with our neighbors and our customers. My grandmother, everybody adored her. And everybody loved my mother because she was my grandmother's daughter!

According to Sarah, her grandmother, Yehudas, or Hanuska Goldner Stern, was quite an important person in the village: family, community leader, and "doctor!" As the town midwife, she assisted at every birth.

DOCTOR STERN: Sarah watches her Grandma delivering a baby.

Lodomir took me a half hour to get to, Svidnik a whole hour. A little girl walking alone in the woods. Someone would ask, "Who are you?"
"I'm Hanuska's granddaughter!"
That's all you needed. She was very well known.

> Grandma told me that, as a little girl, her mother would send her into town to buy a dozen eggs. She would tell her when she had three in each hand, it meant she had six eggs. Another three in each hand meant she had a full dozen.
> - Jerry Zucker

What kind of a name is that?
That's Slovenian.

And your grandmother was also from Hinkovitz?
No, she was born in Verdun. She got to Hinkovitz because somebody knew her, and they knew my grandfather, and they thought they'd make a nice couple. That's how everybody was married. Matchmakers. Her maiden name was Goldner.

And Grandpa's name was Samuel D. (Shlomo David) Stern. The marriages were matched from a great distance.

They must've been! Did she like the guy she married?
We never asked that; we asked, "Did she get married?"

SAMUEL & YEHUDAS: No photographs exist, but these figurines, for years a fixture on the Wildwood fireplace mantel, I imagine reminded Grandma of her own grandparents.

Sarah's Grandmother's parents were Moishe and Fage (Fanny) Goldner. Their children were Yehudas, Dvorah, Hersh Yitzhak, Leah and Moise. Since Yehudas waas the eldest, born c.1830, her mother Fage was most likely born around the time of America's War of 1812. She reportedly lived to 105, but it seems most likely Sarah never met her, since there is no mention of Fage, who may never have set foot in Hinkovitz. Sarah's sister Fanny (Brill) is named for her.

How many children did they have?

They had 12 children, and 10 of the 12 lived, and they all came to America. There were 5 brothers and 3 sisters, and my mother (Rifka) was the oldest. The one I'm named after, Sarah, my mother's younger sister, she died in Passaic. She went to America single. She died in childbirth in Passaic [where she married). I was born in Hinkovitz, she died in Passaic. This is the way it went on.

THE FIGURINES: In the 1940's, center, on the Wildwood Ave. fireplace mantel. My Grandpa Leo Zucker (left) appears to be having a friendly conversation with Frieda's husband, Jack Krasno. The two families shared three duplexes over two decades before Leo and Jack battled each other in a bitter business lawsuit. Krasno won, and the two didn't speak for years, much to the dismay of Sarah and Frieda, who remained close. As the story goes, at Mom and Dad's September 1941 wedding, when Jack appeared at the door, Leo simply said, "It's okay Jack, come in."

> *Nancy Rosten showed me a translation of an 1896 letter, written by Yehudas, clearly not happy about her children leaving for America, particularly complaining that (Nancy's father) Isador, then 17, had not written!*

August 2, 1896

Dearest and much beloved daughter of your mother in law, Malke Stern, and my beloved son, Moshe Stern,

First of all I want to report that all of us are well. We hope to hear the same from you for always and ever, Amen. Second, dear daughter of mother in law, I write that I do not know what to think. I go around only sad because my dear son Israel (Isador) doesn't write. I request from you, my dear child, an answer; write me if he is living, God forbid he is not living. Gurwich wrote me that he has written Israel, but does not receive answers. So please, dear children, write immediately because I don't hear from my children. On the other hand, I have been delighted by your letters, so write to me again, immediately because I don't hear from my children.

As I started this letter to you, a letter arrived from you to me. You cannot imagine my happiness I had and I think you dear child that you delighted me with your sweet script. I wish you mazel-tov that you should live with your lovely husband and son and fulfill many mitzvahs and good deeds and you should get such nachas from your children.

Tell my dear son, Israel, that he should do the same and come home when he can and at that time he will also become a citizen. Maybe Yosef ar Yienkel can take his name. The notary told me he can get a passport claim it. Don't let him do otherwise. Let him come home and do it. If he can return, you should also come (five months later). Do not be afraid, you will find everything as you left it. Just be sure to do it because I have no peace of mind when you are gone. I don't sleep at night until you come. If you don't write and pay attention, the rabbi of Aemanoff, may he long live, told me that I should write to you that you should come home. That immediately when you hold this letter you should write Mense Gurwitz he is also coming home, you should come with him.

I have no more news to tell you dear children when I receive a letter from you I will again write you. I greet you and bless you my dear Malke and my dear son Moshe and your dear children, with life, your true mother who hopes to hear only good news from you and hopes to see you shortly. A hearty blessing from Moshe and Rifka. Her husband and children they also send their regards and now a hearty greeting from me and my children I'll expect letters from you. Dear Stern children, write good letters for you dear mother. Greetings also from the Tzumplish also send regards to all Stern Brothers. Write me back, your dear mother.

2nd reply 5

Rifka her husband and children greet and kiss you. Now I write you my dear and beloved child Israel Stern, your card is held by me with great joy which you wrote in your own handwriting.

Now I write that when you are gone I have no moments of peace and I won't rest until you return. When you return you will find everything as you left. Menshe Gurwitz is also returning home. I write you that we have 3 wagons more of hay than in the previous year. I also have very beautiful Manhearn fruit and vegetables. Bless the Lord, the barn is full with much fodder, but it is difficult to harvest it. My eyes are full of tears since you left and I last spoke to you.

I will free you only if you immediately answer my letter when you receive it. Moshe and Hannah also return home because they cannot make a living elsewhere. Your dear mother lonely to see you soon and in good health.

Malka hugs and kisses you with heartfelt feeling. Greeting from Israel Tzimet and his wife and children to all the Stern brothers. Everyone wishes you a good new year.

You should have the life of Moses Montefiore and the wherewithal of the Rothschilds

STERN DESCENDANTS, 2016: (Nancy Stern Rosten, far right, I'm 3rd from right) "Three wagons full of hay and a barn full of fodder" notwithstanding, generations of American Sterns owe a debt of gratitude to their great grandfather Isador for not listening to his mother.

Did the Stern brothers and sisters all come (to America) before your mother?

Yes, Mother was the last. Her mother (Yehudas) lived a long time, and my mother would not leave her. Then when she died, (early 1900's?) Mother started working on this thing, that she won't go to America because she wants to visit her mother in the cemetery every year. So then we had a problem. She came around in time. She was all right. She was happy she came here.

Where did the rest of the aunts and uncles settle, all over?
Kenosha. Four brothers.

That must have been that family...

That's right. Their father was the youngest of the family. Isador Stern. And there was my mother, and there was Molly Grossman, you've heard the Grossman name.

There was another sister. The five brothers were Joe, Max, Jacob, Joseph, Isador. Four in Kenosha and one in Milwaukee.

STERN FAMILY: "Cousins Club" picnic, Brown's Lake Wisconsin July 1937: Top row: Isador, (father of Nancy Rosten) Joe, Jake, Max. Bottom Row: Morris, Mollie, Rifka, Anna (Max's wife) Rifka, at 81, was the eldest sibling and stand-out fashionista.

> **I know that my Dad came to Milwaukee first because of his brothers. I think Uncle Joe was a peddler around Milwaukee. I guess Uncle Jake was the first one in Kenosha. I really didn't know Uncle Morris, he died when I was young.**
> **- Nancy Stern Rosten**

Do you have any idea where the Surlows came from before they were in Hinkovitz?
The Surlow family came from somewhere around Dukla.

Who was the first in the family to leave?
Uncle Phil was the first one to go. He was first. Then Uncle Sam was here (Milwaukee) they were all here.

Phillip (b. 1881) came to Milwaukee 1899, lived with Max and Hannah Stern in Kenosha. Fannie (b. 1885) emigrated 1900, Lena (b. 1887) emigrated c.1904(?) Sam (b. 1889) emigrated c.1907. Frieda (b. 1891) emigrated 1908.

I was the oldest at home. And he (Uncle Phil) kept writing to say come on. Well, as soon as he could afford it.

So you had to wait for Uncle Phil to send money?
No, not at all. Mother didn't want to go!

Why not?
The main reason was that she couldn't go to the cemetery every year, because on Rosh Hashana and Yom Kippur you go to visit the graves of the departed and she had a father and mother there and two children in that cemetery.

ANNUAL VISIT: Rifka at Lodomir Cemetery

My mother lost two children. The oldest, even older than Uncle Phil, a girl, and the second was born after Uncle Maury - or was it after me? After me, a little girl, and she died.

Would there be a Jewish cemetery there that would say some names of our family?
You mean in the original cemetery? My mother's parents were buried, yes. That would be there, but I would have no way of telling you that it is. I hope it is.

Where would the Hinkovitz cemetery be?
On the way to Svidnik, on this side. A half a mile from our house. It was near Lodomir, the other town that was half a mile from us.

Bob didn't find it. That's a very small village. A little bit larger than Hinkovitz, and mostly Jewish people living there. It was a shtetl.

> *On the 2003 trip, I looked for the cemetery. There were a few cemeteries visible from the road, but they were all attached to churches. Finally, we found a man who told us to look about a half mile up the road and ask the Gypsies. Sure enough, we found the Gypsies a half mile up the road. We got out of the car, and were immediately surrounded by dozens of kids.*

ROCK STAR: My childhood friend Jon Paris, now a well known New York blues guitarist, gave me dozens of picks engraved with "Jon Paris Band." The kids were thrilled at being so close to the friend of a real live American Rock Star.

1979: Jon Paris with rock star Johnny Winter

1964: Jon Paris with rock star David Zucker

> *One of the young men there said he knew the location of the old cemetery was and offered to show us the way. He led us up a steep hill, what seemed like a long climb, but finally, we reached the top and there it was, overgrown, neglected, many of the headstones bent or overturned -- but this was unmistakably, the Lodomir Jewish cemetery Sarah referred to.*

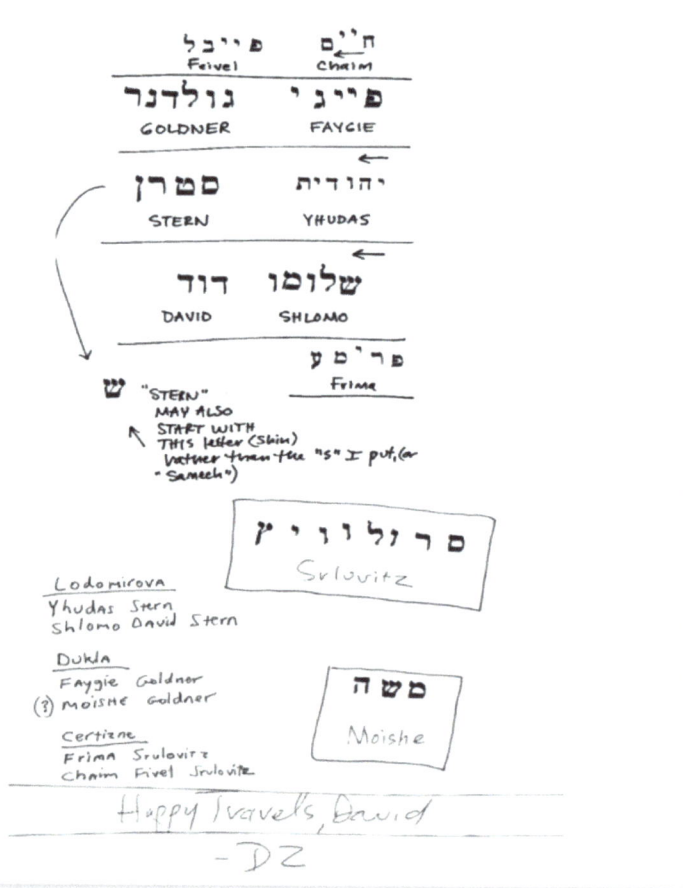

NEEDLE IN A HAYSTACK: Cousin Debbie Zucker had prepared a Hebrew version for me of some of the names that might be on the headstones, but there were hundreds of them; it would have taken me weeks to find it.

LODOMIR CEMETERY 2008: Abandoned and in disrepair, this is one of hundreds of Jewish Cemeteries throughout Europe in need of restoration. A group called The Heritage Foundation is working to restore these sites. As soon as I amass enough money to beable to spend on insane, crazy stuff, I plan to restore the cemetery and go back to find the needle.

And Uncle Phil kept writing. He would write letters, he and Uncle Sam, to say "come on, come here to America." He was happy to be in America. In one, he enclosed a silver dollar and said, "Everything important about America can be found on this coin" Liberty, (freedom) In God We Trust, (founded on religious principles) E Pluribus Unum (Out of many, one Melting Pot). But the letters weren't all positive. They were struggling a bit, to make a living. the winters were very cold. But I left those parts out when I read them to mother, and I guess I probably added other things, positive things, that weren't exactly in the letters. And also a big reason (for Rifka's reluctance) was the kosher.

THIS JUST IN: Sarah reading the latest letter from her brother, using her imaginative powers to embellish the wondrous charms of frozen Milwaukee. I like to think I inherited some of her great fictional storytelling talent.

"If you go to America, you'll surely eat *treif*, and God will not have it, God will punish you." I promised her I would always keep kosher. "If you go to America, when you marry, you won't shave your head. God will not have it. God will punish you." I promised her I would shave my head. "If you go, your grand children will not be Jewish." I promised her they would be Jewish. "Then your great grand children will not be Jewish." And I promised her they would, but she went on.

What made her finally change her mind?
It's that rabbi that made her see - I told you the story about the rabbi – who told her she better go to America with four single daughters and three single sons! He lived in a town not too far away, but on a river…

This river [on the map] that shows here must have been a tributary that went into this larger Svidnik River. Because there was a big river that went from Svidnik…
Yes, it went to Svidnik and from there, to …

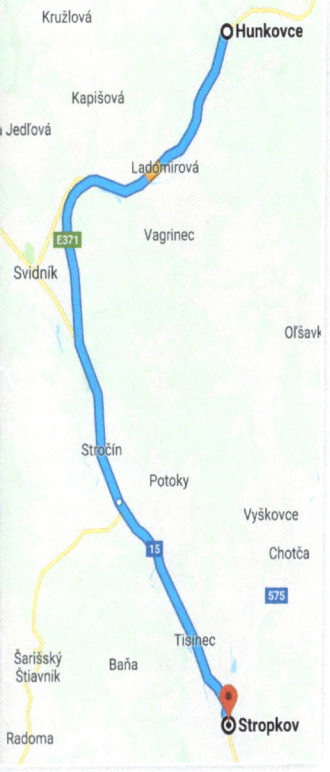

Stropkov? Yeah, here it is. It's the next town on the river here: Stropkov.

You have it there? Oh my God, children, what are you doing? [laughs]

And then from there it went into almost a lake.

Yes. And the water was blue, like the Blue Danube! It was beautiful!

It was five or maybe 10 miles from Stropkov that this lake was.

Yes, yes, yes! I remember the lake, you could see it from Stropkov. I was inStropkov many times. It was Stropkov where this rabbi lived who told my mother to go to America. Yes. He was a smart rabbi and he told her what to do.

THE LAKE AT STROPKOV: About a 15 minute car ride from the town. Exactly as Sarah described it, beautiful!

> *Uncle Bob Zucker told me the story of how anxious Grandma was to leave Hungary, and Rifka kept saying no. In desperation, she went to see the Rabbi in Stropkov.*

SAGE OF STROPKOV: Rabbi Avraham Shalom Halberstam. Jews, learned and simple alike, sought the advice and blessing of this "Miracle Rabbi of Stropkov," revered as a living link in the *chain of Chassidus of Sanz and Sienawa*.

RABBI AVRHAHAM SHALOM HALBERSTAM (1856–1940)

In 1897, Rabbi Halberstam was appointed Rabbi of Stropkov, succeeding Rabbi Yitzhak Hersh Amsel (c1855–1934) who was appointed Rabbi of Zborov. Rabbi Halberstam served in Stropkov for some forty years, until the early 1930s, when he assumed a rabbinical post in the larger town of Košice. Rabbi Menachem Mendel Halberstam (1873–1954), the son of the aforementioned Rabbi Avraham Shalom Halberstam was then appointed chief rabbi of Stropkov and head of the Talmud Torah till WWII. Thank God for the internet.

> Your grandmother had a problem. She's sixteen years old, everyone she knew, friends, relatives, everyone had left that little town. She missed her brothers and sister, her father had left, and her mother, my grandmother, just refused to go. So she decided to ask a rabbi, a very learned man, for advice on what to do. She was at her wits end. So she traveled to a nearby village where this rabbi lived, and told him of her dilemma. According to Grandma, this rabbi, after a long pause, leaned in to her and asked, "Sarah… are you willing to tell a white lie?" Grandma, at first taken by surprise, said "Yes, yes, I think so." And the Rabbi told her, "Alright, this is what you should do. Tell your mother that your beschert (intended husband) is waiting for you in America!"
> - Bob Zucker

BEFORE THE INVENTION OF SMILING

THE THREE RABBIS: The oil painting above the mantle in this 1956 photo, one of many that Sarah collected, was for many years in the home of my Aunt Clarice (Ecy) Zucker, who has since donated it to Chabad Lubevitch of Milwaulkee. It's been adapted for this book, as I imagine it could have reminded Grandma of her meeting with Rabbi Halberstam.

> **"**
> So she left Stropkov, full of hope -- after the Rabbi gave her the advice on how to deal with her mother - and that's exactly what she did – she repeated the rabbi's optimistic prediction to Rifka. Of course, she added for good measure, that if she stayed in Hinkovitz, she would wind up marrying one of the local peasant boys. Grandma didn't need any more convincing!
> - Bob Zucker
> **"**

So, when did you finally leave?
It was in the Summer. From Hinkovitz we went to Dukla - that's Poland.

> *From the Ellis Island records, the family probably departed Hinkovitz in late July of 1909.*

We sent (Aunt Bee and Uncle Maury) ahead with a truck that delivered - a covered wagon, we called them trucks - that delivered onions maybe from Dukla to some Austrian city, and came past Hinkovitz, and they knew us and we knew them. They used to stop in overnight. And so we told them our story of woe, and they said "we'll help you; take the two youngsters with us and you walk." Because nobody would bother about the youngsters in the covered wagon. They'd think they were your children.

THE TRUNK: *All the family's belongings (whatever they could carry) were packed in a trunk and loaded onto the covered wagon. The trunk is one of only a few items which survive from Hinkovitz. Sarah gave the trunk to her daughter-in-law, my aunt, Eve Joan Zucker, who had it restored, changing the original black to green. She passed it on to me in the late 1990's. It's now in my living room. (above) I do think the green looks better.*

And you had to sneak over the border?

Yes. Or else they would take everything away that you had with you. If you had any money on you, or ... passage, tickets. But we had a passport, we did have that. Uncle Phil and Uncle Sam sent passage to us. My father was here already. He also went with people in a covered wagon. He didn't have to walk like we did. They just took him along like he was going on business. Father had a passport. How he got it, I don't ever know. Whether he had help, I don't know.

But they would suspect you, because you wouldn't be going on business?
Yeah, and too many local people would have known about it.

You kept it a secret and didn't sell your house, then?
That's right. We left our house to a relative of ours. He was a young man, and we left everything there. Eventually he was supposed to pay us, when he did well in our store, in our building. He was some distant relative of my father's. And then when the first World War broke out, 1914, he was called to the army. He was a young married man. And he had to go … and he never came back. We never heard from him again, or from his family. None of us have ever gone back.

TEMPORARY PARTING: The family traveled together in the wagon for a few miles until Sarah and Rifka had to strike off on their own through the woods to the border.

How did you manage to get across the border?
We had to walk through the woods all night. Just Mother and me. We came through the woods on foot. We knew the way, so we walked all night. A rainy night.

Mother was 53 and I was 16. It was a lonely night, a fearful night. We avoided going too near any of the houses, we were always afraid someone would see us.

So how long did it take for you to walk from Hinkovitz to Dukla? We made it overnight. We walked through the woods, through birches and pines. A couple of stops to rest, but we were afraid to go into any house or anything - everything was dark. It took us the whole night. We walked a pretty good pace. Mother was in good shape, her health was good. There was no question about it. There was a drizzle all the way to Dukla, so that interfered. And Mother provided sugar candy - I don't know how she - she had pockets full. In her dress, her purse. She filled everything with candy, cookies, something to help us.

BIRCHES AND PINES: In the woods leading to the Polish border. In the background is an artillery piece, a remnant of the 1944 Battle of Dukla Pass.

What did you take with you?
Nothing at all. We sent everything with these people in the covered wagon. We had the cards. I had that and all the money - I don't remember how much. A couple of thousand dollars Hungarian money. I had that sewed into my bra. It was sewed into a pocket, flat. And then on the side under my arm in my bra. And that's the way I carried it, all the way to America.

And Aunt Bee and Uncle Maury?
We crossed through the town and looked for the synagogue. After a short walk, we found the synagogue and reunited with Aunt Bee and Uncle Maury.

DUKLA, 2008: The building, and others in the town square, date from the 19th century.

RENDEZVOUS POINT: The Dukla Synagogue, 1909 and today.

How old were Aunt Bee and Uncle Maury?
They don't like me to tell, so don't tell them about it. They like to tell people they were born here, but I don't see what there is to cover. [Laughs] Uncle Maury was 12 and Bee was I think 7. Because I think what are we here, since nineteen-nine -67 years or 68? Uncle Maury will be 80 on his next birthday. I say he is 79 and leave it at that, but he was 12 when he came here.

> *Bertha (Bee) Surlow was born July 22, 1900. Morris (Maury) was born two years earlier, on October 13, 1898, which would have made him 11 when the family emigrated, Bee 9. According to a family story, Morris was born with a different name, Shmuel, and renamed after a childhood accident. Apparently, older brother Phil accidentally "put him into a scythe," leaving him with a huge scar on his left leg. The rabbi from Lodomir was summoned, said a bracha, and advised that he be henceforth named after a person in the Torah who lived a long time: Moishe, (Moses) who lived for 120 years! Shmuel became his middle name, hence, "M.S. Surlow (Maurice Samuel)*

So he had his Bar Mitzvah the next year?
Yes, here. He had his Hebrew training in Europe, but he took some more here, and Bee was born in 1900, so she will now be - July - she won't give me the date -but we came here in 1909. And from there, we were taken with horse and wagon to Krakow.

We stayed in Krakow three days - Friday, Saturday, and Sunday - Mother wouldn't travel on Saturdays.

Little did she know, she'll get to America, she'll have to. But she never did. She refused it. But we traveled to Amsterdam, where we embarked several days later.

You went by wagon all that way?
No, a train. Once we got to Krakow, we were to continue traveling by train, but we were there for three days, because Mother had to stay. She was worried that if we didn't stay there, we wouldn't make it to the next stop by Friday. She had candles with her.

> Grandma once told me the story behind the brass candlesticks. Evidently they were a gift from Isaac to Rifka in 1900, when Rifka was pregnant. Since she had already given him four girls, and three boys, Isaac hoped that his next arrival would be a boy. So toward the end of the pregnancy, on one of his buying trips to Budapest, Isaac purchased a fine pair of brass candlesticks to reward his wife. When he returned, he found that Rifka had given birth to a baby girl (Aunt Bee). "But", Grandma related, "He gave her the candlesticks anyway!"
> - Michael Zucker

SHABBAT IN KRAKOW: Stayed the night in the hotel.

THE CANDLESTICKS TODAY: One of only a few surviving Srulovitz possessions from Hungary, now on display in my den, surrounded by Mom and Dad's glass collection. On the top shelf is a ship model, crafted by Dad in a 1930 shop class. Throughout my childhood, it was a fixture on my bedroom shelf.

BLESSING THE CANDLES: The prayer shawl is seen in this late 1930's photograph, and as it appears today in my home with the Menorah. According to the photographer, Aunt Bee, taking a picture of Mom on Shabbat in mid-prayer was not appreciated.

RIFKA'S PRAYER SHAWL: Here, worn by my mother, Charlotte, in this carefully posed 1950's photo. We blessed candles every Friday night, but my mother never wore a head scarf, shawl or put her hands to her face. Years later, in the early 2000's, when Dad was in the Milwaukee Jewish Home, Mom would smuggle bacon up to his room.

So, if you had to wait in Krakow for three days, weren't you worried you would miss the boat?

It didn't matter. Mother insisted. "This is the way it's got to be; this is the way God wants it." She was never without God for a second, never until the day she died. And I think it's a good idea. Keep God alongside. You have no one else, you might as well bring God.

KRAKOW TRAIN STATION, 1909.

So then you boarded the train at the Krakow station?

Yes.

Was that where Aunt Bee and Uncle Maury immediately started turning on the faucets? **Oh, yes!** [laughs] It was the first time they had ever seen running water! We couldn't stop them!

What was the train ride like?
We had to be very watchful. When Mother slept, I stayed awake. And when I slept *she* stayed awake, so nobody could touch (the hidden money) it. There were all kinds of thieves on the trains and on the boat. And they knew that they saw an old lady and a young girl. Who knows? Maybe the old lady, maybe the young girl has some money on her or jewelry or something. We left for America from Rotterdam.

So the train took you to Rotterdam? Or Amsterdam?
It was one of the two. I am confused between the two. It was a German place. We waited there for a few days in a hotel. I spoke German when I went to the bank to get some cash. It was Plottdeutsch. They were dressed like the Dutch people.

> *The Ellis Island Manifest records show the ship, The Kaiser Wilhelm, departed from Bremen, Germany. So definitely "a German place."*

And there you got on a ship?
Yes. Everything was assigned to us.

Did you have to go steerage?
No no no no no. First class. My brother Phil wouldn't have it steerage.

> *A check of the Ellis Island manifest indicates that the Srulovitz party was in steerage. Sarah, proud as she was, may have conveniently forgot.*

PRINZ FRIEDRICH WILHELM: Built in 1908 for Bremen - New York service. Given as war reparations to Canada in 1921 and renamed Empress of China. Subsequently renamed Empress of India, 1922, Montlaurier, 1923, Monteith, 1925, and Montnairn, 1926. After all the renamings, scrapped in Italy in 1930.

BEFORE THE INVENTION OF SMILING

> " I remember Uncle Maury telling me how the first class passengers on the ship used to throw pennies down to the steerage kids below, for sport. The kids then would all pile in a mad scramble for the the pennies or nickels or whatever they were throwing..
> - Debbie Zucker "

STEERAGE KIDS: Whether or not Bee and Maury participated in this wild scrambling for money, I'd bet Grandma, with her strong sense of family pride and ambition, would have stopped them. "We're better than this. Someday *we're* going to be up there!" Or not.

So when you first arrived, you came to NY?
Yes, we were only in New York for one day, thank God for that [Laughs]. We knew we were heading to Milwaukee. We stopped in New York and in Chicago. I had heard about the Statue of Liberty ... mother cried and I cried when we saw that.

AMERICA: She hadn't seen her sister, Fanny and brother, Phil, for 10 years.

PART TWO
AMERICA

AMERICA

THE GLOBE NEWSPAPER, SEPTEMBER 29, 1909: Barely a month after Sarah's arrival, Wilbur Wright flew around the Statue of Liberty. More than one million New Yorkers witnessed the flight, which lasted approximately 33 minutes and covered 20 miles. In case of an emergency, Wilbur attached a canoe to the bottom of the plane!

BEFORE THE INVENTION OF SMILING

Did you have to go through Ellis Island?
Yes, I saw something not long ago about it.

ELLIS ISLAND PROCESSING CENTER: Srulovitz family at upper right, near head of the line.

They were interviewing people . . . I could've been interviewed and given the same answer. But this man's memory was better. He was a bit older. I was occupied. I had Mother to look after. And a younger brother and sister to look after, and I had to do the talking for everyone.

S.S. PRINZ FRIEDRICH WILHELM SAILING FROM BREMEN AUG 3, 1909.

	NAME IN FULL	AGE YRS. MOS.	SEX	MARRIED OR SINGLE	CALLING OR OCCUPATION
SZURLOVITS	REGINA	50	F	MARRIED	HOUSEWIFE
""	SAROLTA	15 1/2	F	SINGLE	CHILD
""	SAMUEL	8 1/2	M	SINGLE	""
""	BETI	7 1/2	F	SINGLE	""

ABLE TO - READ	WRITE	NATIONALITY	RACE OR PEOPLE	LAST PERMINANT RESIDENCE	THE NAME & COMPLETE ADDRESS OF NEAREST RELATIVE OR FRIEND	FINAL DESTINATION STATE/ CITY
N	N	HUNGARY	HEBREW	HUNGARY	WIFE REGINA SZURLOVITS	WISC./MILWAUKEE
Y	Y	""	""	""	""	""
Y	Y	""	""	""	""	""
Y	Y	""	""	""	""	""

A CLOSER LOOK: Regina (Rifka), Sarolta (Sarah), Beti (Bee) and Samuel (Maury) setting sail on the SS Prinz Friedrich Wilhelm from Bremen on August 3rd, 1909. They arrived at the Port of New York on August 12, 1909. 7 days later, Sarah would turn 16 years old.

BEFORE THE INVENTION OF SMILING

What was your impression of New York?
I didn't like what I saw because I saw Hester Street.

EVEN MILWAUKEE WAS BETTER: Hester Street c. 1909.

I was not accustomed to living that way. It was a slum. In Europe we lived very well. We had a lovely house, a lot of land. And we were dressed well. My father was a businessman in Europe; he had a dry goods store there. General store. Dry goods and groceries. We would dress like we dress here, maybe not as expensive, but … what I saw in New York I did not like. I thought, I'll come to Milwaukee and I'll take a look and I'll say, I want to go back. And I did!

> *Sarah was most likely referring to some subsequent trip to New York, which evidently at the time was worthy of a news story.*

Mr. and Mrs. Leo Zucker, Highland avenue, have left for a trip to New York. They will return by way of Canada where they will visit with friends.

WISCONSIN JEWISH CHRONICLE: 1927

> *Steerage passengers were ferried directly from Ellis Island to Jersey City, where the family would have boarded a train to Chicago.*

CENTRAL RAILROAD OF NEW JERSEY TERMINAL: Or Jersey City Terminal, was the Central Railroad of New Jersey's waterfront passenger terminal. The current terminalbuilding, now overgrown with plants, its tracks lost beneath foliage, was in operation from 1889 until it was abandoned in 1967.

INDIANA: What train travel looked like in the first decade of the 20th century.

From Chicago, we boarded another train to Milwaukee. When we arrived, the first thing I saw was the Northwestern Depot. Do you remember the Northwestern Depot before it was torn down? **Yeah.**

CHICAGO & NORTHWESTERN RAILWAY DEPOT, MILWAUKEE, 1909: Although it was a letdown for Sarah, who had seen more magnificent architecture in Europe, it was nonetheless, the historical entry point for many Milwaukee families. Built entirely of stone in 1889, it was a wonderful example of 19th century Romanesque style with a clock tower that reached 234 feet. Sadly, it was demolished in 1967 to make way for a freeway that was then never built, a double tragedy.

SPEAKING OF DOUBLE TRAGEDY: The old Milwaukee Road Depot, a wonderful example of 19th century Gothic Revival, designed by well-known architect Edward Townsend Mix, boasted the largest clock tower in America (140 feet) at the time of its construction in 1886. Incredibly, after a 1985 fire, it was torn down and replaced by this architectural abortion:

MILWAUKEE UNION STATION 1966: I try to put this image out of my mind, like the scene in the 1989 movie "Glory" where a soldier gets his head blown off by a cannonball. Nonetheless, I have fantasies of lining up the architect along with the city officials responsible for this travesty in front of a rifle squad and yelling "FIRE!"

And I thought, This is America? This is Milwaukee and this is where I'm going to live? Oh no! I had already been in depots in big cities in Europe. But I accepted it because I was excited, because I expected Uncle Phil and Uncle Sam to come. But I guess they misunderstood us. We sent the wire from New York to tell them when we were coming in, but they came a bit late. Not too late, but we wanted them to be there.

Did you call them?
From the North Western Depot I called Aunt Fanny's house. She was married five years then and she already had two children, and she had a telephone on the wall that you had to crank.

Did you have to go through the operator?
I went through the operator because I didn't know how to call the number in English. 592 Fifth Street. I'll never forget that address.

CHICAGO & NORTHWESTERN DEPOT: Where Sarah made her call to the Brills.

I asked the girl at the desk in the depot if she spoke German, and she said "Yawoll." I said "Can you help me get the telephone number for 592 Fifth Street?" in German. I can still do it - I never speak German, but it never leaves you, what you learn when you're young. I was young, very healthy with rosy cheeks. I suppose she admired me. We were all very healthy. It shows you now, we go on living until into the 80s and God knows what. And she called the number for me and she gave me the receiver and I didn't know what to do. She told me to hold this part to my ear and I'll hear a sound.

Pretty soon there was an uncle at Uncle Joe's (Brill's) place. They had a duplex and the factory was upstairs and the living quarters were down. They had a man by the name of Mandelbaum who lived with them; he was a widower and lived there for very many years. He was a cutter, a trimmer in their factory. He was the everything: the shipping clerk, he answered the phone, he did everything.

That's what the Brills grew into now. He answered the phone. I said: "Is this the Brill's home?" He said "Yes, who is this?" I said "This is Mrs. Brill's sister."
So he right away connected me. He must have known we were coming, and he knew I can't speak English.

He called, I think, Aunt Fanny, and she came and cried. That's the first thing you do. I hardly remembered her. I was very little when she left Europe.

> *Fanny, 24, had emigrated in 1900 at the age of 15, when Sarah was 7, originally staying, as Phil had, with Max and Hannah Stern in Kenosha, in 1899, when Maury was barely a year old. It's possible Fanny may have been in Hinkovitz for the birth of Bee, but this would be the first time Phil would meet his youngest sister, now 9.*

I didn't remember Uncle Phil at all. I remembered Uncle Sam and Frieda.

Because they left later?
Yes. She apologized [for crying] and I cried too. Then I told her that we just arrived to the North Western Depot. She said she had the telegram and Phil and Sam are on the way to meet me. And so I went back to sit next to Mother and I gave her the report. I did all the traveling for Mother and Bee and Uncle Maury.

BEFORE THE INVENTION OF SMILING

We went out on Grand Ave, it wasn't called Wisconsin Avenue yet, and waited for Uncle Phil and Uncle Sam.

And the first thing you saw was the Elk's Club?
No, the Elk's Club was not there! There's a post office now and an Elk's Club. It was a little box - there was some guy, and he had a few hot dogs for sale there. Maybe ice cream. But I saw the cover over the top in case it rained, or for sun too.

AMERICA

I'm so sorry they did away with that building. It was my marker. A lot of people were sorry. And I walked out of there . . .

How long had it been since you 'd seen the last relative? Who was last?
Aunt Frieda came in 1908.

You hadn't seen Aunt Frieda for a year? And Uncle Sam?
He came in 1907. Two years.

Your father?
He came the same year we did - three or four months before us. We came in August. He came in the Spring. I cried when I saw Frieda. She shocked me. She was always a pretty healthy specimen; pretty heavy, well-built. And they brought her home from the store where she was working, and I didn't recognize her. She had lost so much weight. She had a very hard time. The people she lived with took advantage of her. She was very sick.

How did she get mixed in with these people?
Well, she had to live somewhere. She had no place to live so she boarded with these people. She earned six dollars a week. She paid room and board three dollars. She had very little to live on. They made her do housework nights. They took advantage of her. She worked all day, hard. She had a harder time with language than I did. It took her a while before she caught on to the English. And she didn't speak Hungarian or German. She spoke Yiddish and Slovenian.

We had a house on on Fourth and Vliet St. waiting for us. And we lived there only a year or two. I took you there one day. But the house is no more. The four-family apartment was cleared away. I so wanted you to see that, but there was a parking lot there or something.

A PARKING LOT OR SOMETHING: 4TH & Vliet today: (317 Vliet)

We cashed [our European money] in here. It was so much less here - a dollar was worth 2 1/2 gulden. When they used to send us a $10 bill, we'd get 25 dollars, our money. I had so much when I left Europe . . . when it was changed into American money [chuckles]. . . but we still had enough to open up grocery stores and go into business. My father found this place on Walnut St. for a grocery store. Six room apartment upstairs. We moved there. We doubled up. Three boys slept in one bedroom. The girls, four in one bedroom - a good-sized room.

LETS JUST KEEP THE OLD AWNING: 8th and Walnut, Milwaukee. Isaac bought the business from Max Fairman in 1910. Left to right: sisters Lena, Bee and Sarah. The sign on the glass door reads: "P.H. Srulovitz & Bro Groceries."

Aunt Frieda came to live with us right away. My mother felt terrible. And we opened a business in the Yiddish neighborhood, (3rd&) Walnut Street, where we could talk Yiddish, and there were a lot of Slovak people and Polish people.

All kinds of foreigners. The town was full of foreign Jews from all over. That's when time opened up for everybody to come here. 19 . . . was it 1905 when it opened up, and we came here 1909? In 1905, I guess, America opened up to foreigners.

How about the rest of the people who came?
Uncle Sam peddled for a short while but he didn't do well; he didn't like it. He spoke the languages fairly well, he got around. He could take care of himself. He got a job at Schuster's on 12th and Vliet in the window shade department. All he had to do was measure for windows in different homes, and fit the shades on the roller and deliver them. So that he did for quite some time, and before you knew it, he was in business for himself - he had a store in West Allis and he did very well. Uncle Phil had a liquor store near there too, before they both moved to Los Angeles.

UNCLE PHIL, WEST ALLIS, 1946: The CinZano rooster, [inset] originally from this store, was a longtime fixture on the Wildwood Ave. basement bar. It now lives on *my* bar, and according to Dad, reminded Grandpa Leo of the rooster who thought the sun came up because *he* crowed.

AMERICA

THE WALNUT ST. GROCERY STORE: Bee, Rifka, Isaac and Sam at 628 Walnut St. In that era, a photographer might pass by in a wagon, stop and offer to take a photograph for 25 cents, which he would develop on the spot.

SITE OF THE GROCERY STORE, 2021: Now occupied by vast tracts of low rise warehouses, hospitals and parking lots, no trace exists of the former immigrant neighborhood. For miles in each direction, there was no structure I could find dating from before even 1960. I imagine a pre-1945 resident of Hiroshima, returning today, would have the same experience.

BEFORE THE INVENTION OF SMILING

Walnut Street Historic Photo Collection / Milwaukee Public Library, Str.Walnut.Pre1960.017

WALNUT STREET, c. 1929: The 700 block of Walnut Street, this appears to be one of the few photographs of the area pre-1970's. Future Israeli Prime Minister Golda Meir and her parents lived at 623 Walnut St. and are listed in the 1908 through 1910 directories.

WALNUT STREET, 2021: The 700 block today.

It was hardship, but always with a smile. Nobody ever complained. Nobody ever cried. We always wound up by saying, "Thank God we're in America. God's country." Also, it was good to be together with the family. We had Uncle Max living in West Allis - he had a big family, 10 or 12 children. They're all still around. You know Sarah Stern who was here who died not long ago? And Hattie Stern. There was a judge, a lawyer, a dentist Stern. Big family. They all had a college education and did well. They were our family. Their father was my mother's brother. And he was helpful to us.

Cowalsky & Co. Historic Photo Collection / Milwaukee Public Library, RW1267PC

CHARLES COWALSKY & CO. LIVERY: 605 - 609 Walnut January 1910. Rifka most likely was taken by surprise by this huge snowstorm, since it's likely Sarah conveniently skipped any mention of the brutal Milwaukee weather described in Uncle Sam's letters.

My mother didn't have a problem wherever she was. She was a good cook, good baker, and a happy woman because she always had God on her side.

SUPERMARKET, 1910: Rifka in the Walnut St. Grocery store.

And she had lovely children that she was very proud of. And you couldn't do anything, I mean you couldn't do anything to hurt her or to make her feel sorry for coming here.

WITH GOD ON HER SIDE: Not appearing at all sorry to be in America, Rifka holds on to a new fangled automobile, accompanied by Bee on the running board, and half of Maury's face at the hood.

How long did it take you and your mother to feel that you liked America?

Well, not too long. I got around with my relatives. We went to Kenosha, and I visited the father of these people, of Stanley (Nancy Rosten's brother) who was here the other day. His father, Uncle Isador (Stern) was my mother's youngest brother. And he was very good to me. So I'd go to Kenosha often. I'd go to West Allis often. This was all by a streetcar. They'd just given up horse-drawn cars when we came here.

STERN DRY GOODS STORE, KENOSHA: Rifka's brother, Max Stern and his son.

> I wasn't there, but your Grandma (Sarah) and siblings came to Kenosha to have lunch with my Dad and brother (McDonalds guy before McDonalds) Uncle Joe was kosher so he wouldn't go for lunch, but I'm sure they visited with him. Uncle Morris had passed away. Uncle Jake was a little odd, but he was the first Jew in Kenosha and the richest. Anyway, they started talking about ages and Sarah told her age. My Brother said "Dad, that is your age!" Sarah said, "Don't be ridiculous, you were grown up when I was a baby!" Dad wanted to shut her up. I can hear the laughter.
> - Nancy Stern Rosten

THE HINKOVITZ STERN BROTHERS: TOP ROW L to R: (unidentified) Joe, Jake. BOTTOM ROW: Morris, Isadore, Max. The Stern brothers began the family's emigration to America in the early 1880s and settled in Kenosha. This formal portrait was taken in Europe, most likely in a larger town, like Svidnik, which could support a formal studio, complete with fake backdrop. No one seems to have bothered to crop the left side of this one.

A streetcar all the way to Kenosha, or is that the *North Shore Line?* There was a North Shore Line to Kenosha, and a streetcar all the way to West Allis, but that took ages. It stopped on every corner, and the stopping and starting took so long. And I used to go out there every Sunday to be with that family. They were all a bunch of good-looking people. Clean-looking, well-educated, and they were all very warm, very friendly. None spoke a word of Yiddish. They spoke English only. And there I was with all these languages that were no good to me at all. I had to work on English.

But Sam was very good to me; he was the judge.

A BUNCH OF GOOD LOOKING PEOPLE:
Judge Samuel D. Stern, West Allis.

He was in law school then. He tried to help me with my English. And his sister Sarah did. So I used to spend the whole day Sunday with them. That was away from everything, being away from the family and everybody and just being with my new cousins. And my new uncle and aunt who I never knew. I had seen pictures and read letters from them, but I never met them. Uncle Max and all the other brothers came here before I was ever born. It made it very interesting. As soon as I learned to speak such as I did. The people I worked with were foreigners themselves, so there was no one to learn from.

HAKADIMA CLUB, CEDAR LAKE: A Synagogue sponsored gathering of eligible young immigrant singles (c. 1912) includes Sarah and her sister, Frieda [inset] Luckily for me she didn't settle for any of these clowns.

THE FOUR SISTERS c. 1912. From left: Lena, Sarah, Fanny, Frieda.

My father had a grocery store. He bought a nice piece of property on 8th St. (& Walnut) Two properties - on 8th, and North Ave. My mother had the income from it and he also had bonds that he bought. So we did all right. We lived well. Uncle Sam bought a car, a Ford.

UNCLE SAM'S FORD c. 1912. With Aunt Bee pretending to drive.

I married a guy who bought a car. When I got married my husband bought me a vacuum cleaner. That was so unlike us. I was only here five years in this country when we were married.

How did you meet Grandpa?
I met him through Aunt Betty. Aunt Betty and Frieda Montag, who worked in the same place where I worked. So they wanted me to meet their brother, Leo Zucker.

When his Father, Samuel Zucker, came to Milwaukee, he had gone peddling from farm to farm in a horse and wagon. And then from there, when he made enough money, he rented a store on the south side (Milwaukee), on Beecher Street, and he had a dressed goods and dry goods store.

> Regarding Samuel Zucker, I've attached a city directory list for Samuel (and Leo) Zucker from 1909-1917. (I started with 1909, as that was the first year they appeared in the directory.) As you can see, they lived at several different addresses during this time, and I have been working on trying to trace what happened to that particular building/address over time. So far, I know that 548 5th Street became 1638 North 5th Street in 1931. In 1931, a woman named Ida Peters lived at that address. Via google maps, it looks like the houses in that location are no longer standing (although I noticed the location is within a stone's throw of the school Golda Meir attended). I've also been able to determine that 477 7th Street became 1453/1455/1457 North 7th Street. In the early 1930s a barber named William Williams lived there. Through google maps, there is a 1443 North 7th Street building (looks like an apartment building built in the 1960s or so), but nothing that indicates any older buildings located on that block.
> - Jay Hyland
> Archives Director, Jewish Museum Milwaukee

AMERICA

HERBERT HOOVER COLLAR: Leo, looking quite dashing in this 1914 portrait, in all likelihood, irresistible to Grandma.

Where was Grandpa Leo from?
Russia, a little town called Ustilla.

Could this be it, [on the map] this Ustilla?
Right.

That's it? Here it is right here.

BEFORE THE INVENTION OF SMILING

USTILLA, RUSSIA.

That's where Grandpa Leo came from. That's where he was born. He attended Yeshiva there.

And his family was there for how many years?
A long, long time. Many generations.

What did his father do there?
Like he did when he came here, he went peddling. Dressed goods and dry goods, like men's underwear and ladies' underwear.

AMERICA

THE LAX FAMILY IN RUSSIA: Leo's mother, Razel, with her parents, Grandpa David Lax and Grandma Sobol in Ustilla, Russia. Razel died in 1904, four years before her son, Leo, and husband Samuel emigrated. Once in America, Samuel remarried, and the Lax family moved to Hamilton, Ontario where they started a scrap iron business.

YESHIVA, USTILLA, 1903: Young Leo Zucker, 5th row, 9th from right.

I wonder if any Zuckers would still be there (Ustilla)?
I don't think so. If anybody would be there it would be a Montag. Because the Montags' mother was Grandpa Samuel Zucker's sister. Not a Zucker that I know of. After all, I'm an in-law. Grandpa Samuel came here many years ahead of us. He came alone. From Ustilla he had a shorter trip than we did. He became a widower in Europe.

BEFORE THE INVENTION OF SMILING: Leo's Bar Mitzvah in Ustilla, Russia 1905, with his father, Samuel.

He left his children with his parents - with Grandma Sobol and Grandpa David. I say that from hearsay. I never lived there. I didn't know them in Europe and then after he was here for a few years and he peddled and made a few dollars, he brought the rest of the children. Two at a time. Six of them. Their life was very much harder than ours.

Here or in Europe?

Well, here only because their stepmother made it hard. He remarried here, Grandpa Samuel did, to Dr. Leo Weinshel's grandmother. And the stepmother made a hard life, but then I took over when I came into the family. I was glad he (Samuel) was here. I was mad about him. He was the nicest old man you ever knew. He was kind, he was sweet, he was like a father to me. You're named after him. When I married Grandpa (Leo). They all came to live with us.

> *Dr. Leo Weinshel and my father, Burt, were contemporaries. Their fathers, Eddie Weinshel and Leo Zucker, were partners in a pants manufacturing business. This cloth label and business card has survived.*

In the Summer of 1957 I met Leo Weinshel's son, Joe, at a Milwaukee summer camp. We became friends, having only a vague notion of how our families were connected.

AFTER INVENTION OF SMILING: Third Generation. With Joe Weinshel on a recent trip to Milwaukee.

Why did Grandpa's family choose Milwaukee? Did they know the Sterns?

No. These two families had nothing to do with each other. I don't know, through some coincidence. There was a Maury Zucker too. By some recommendation they came to New York. And a lot of people in New York would say, "Why don't you go West? Isn't this crowded?

AMERICA

THE SAMUEL ZUCKER FAMILY. C. 1915: Leo, the visiting Max Lax, his young daughter, Samuel, Frieda & Harry Montag. TOP ROW: Milton, Esther, Betty, Ben.

MODEST BUT TIDY: The Samuel Zucker home, 24th & Burnham.

> Grandpa Sam Zucker's (Leo's dad) store and house were on the corner of 24th and Burnham in Milwaukee. He lived upstairs of the store. Dad and I went to see it and it was in a very modest but tidy neighborhood, and was a very plain white clapboard house.
>
> - Debbie Zucker

They must've thought that's what all of America was.
If you lived in New York, you lived in America, that's it. There was no other part of America. And if you were going to America people would say, "Say hello to my brother, Jack, and tell him we miss him." And God knows what state he lived in.

What was Grandpa's job at that time?
After he came here in 1908, he worked as a laborer in a tannery, then after that he began peddling household goods in a wagon - to the farmers. Eventually, he saved enough money to start his own store. But before that he started a pants manufacturing business with Leo Weinshel's father.

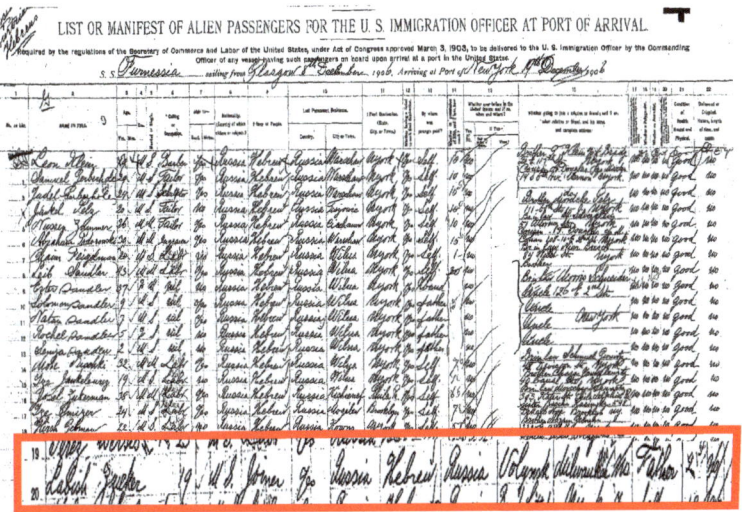

S.S. FURNESSIA SAILING FROM GLASGOW 8TH DEC, 1906. ARRIVING AT PORT OF NEW YORK 19TH DEC, 1906

NAME IN FULL	AGE YRS. MOS.	SEX	MARRIED OR SINGLE	CALLING OR OCCUPATION	ABLE TO -		NATIONALITY	RACE OR PEOPLE	LAST PERMINANT RESIDENCE
					READ	WRITE			
ZUCKER, LABISH	19	M	SINGLE	JOINER	Y	Y	RUSSIA	HEBREW	RUSSIA, VOLNYSK

FINAL DESTINATION	WHETHER HAVING TICKET TO SUCH FINAL DESTINATION	BY WHOM WAS PASSAGE PAID?	WHETHER IN POSSESSION OF $50 AND IF LESS, HOW MUCH?	WHETHER EVER BEFORE IN THE UNITED STATES? AND IF SO, WHEN AND WHERE?	WHETHER GOING TO JOIN A RELATIVE OR FRIEND AND HIS NAME AND COMPLETE ADDRESS
MILWAUKEE, WI	NO	FATHER	2	NO	FATHER M. ZUCKER 1017 GALINE ST

Who is LABISH?: "Labish" Americanized to Leo after he arrived in Milwaukee.

So what was your first date with Grandpa?
He took me down to the theater where they had . . . what do you call that stage show that people are . . .

Vaudeville?
Vaudeville. I couldn't think of the word. I'm slipping kids, I'm slipping. You better get all of this you want [laughs] because I'm slipping. He took me to vaudeville.

THE MARX BROTHERS?: Majestic Theatre, Grand Ave. Milwaukee 1908.

And from there he took me to what was the Schlitz Palm Garden, where you did *not* take girls that young!

Cause they had drinks there?

THE BAR THAT MADE MILWAUKEE FAMOUS: The Schlitz Palm Garden opened as a beer and music hall in 1896 at N. 3rd St. and Grand Ave. (now Wisconsin Ave.) It was razed in 1967.

But he brought me there, and they stopped us at the door and wanted to know how old I was. By that time I must have been about 17 years. 18? 17 or 18. And we were hesitant. You know the Eder family? Olga Eder's father... Olga's maiden name was Donner. They were related to the actor Donner from many years ago, incidentally. And he saw me - he didn't know Grandpa, but he knew I was a Srulowitz girl - and he saw them questioning us at the door.

He seemed to know the people there, and he says, "What do you want? Don't worry about her. I'll vouch for her." So they let us in.

SCHLITZ PALM GARDEN 1911.

We were sitting there, and Grandpa ordered a beer, and I ordered soda water because I wasn't supposed to know how to drink beer. [laughs]. And he's staring at me and staring at me . . . yes, I was 18, it was two years after I came here.

He asked me how old I was. I told him. He said well, what's the difference? If you're not 18, so maybe you're 20. Maybe you don't remember. I didn't like that. I said I know I'm 18. As a matter fact, I wasn't 18 yet. This was in June and my birthday's in August. I said I'm 18. I could've passed for 25!

Were you talking in German or English?
I could handle it all right if it wasn't too much for me. Or I could switch. In the Schlitz Palm Garden you could talk all you wanted in German because they sang in German and they had performances there, everything was done in German. In Milwaukee you could go on the streetcar and talk German to anybody. It was a Deutschland!

What was Grandpa most fluent in?
Hebrew and nobody used it, so that's out. He attended yeshiva in Russia. But here he didn't talk with anybody in Hebrew. And he spoke Yiddish after a fashion and he spoke Polish cause he lived in[?]. He got along in English all right. He mispronounced like I do. People understood as long as he could pay his bill [laughs].

So then what happened?
He took me home. We took the streetcar down, but we walked home, straight up 3rd Street, all the way to Walnut. I thanked him.

He asked for a date. I said "all right."

For that date, he was late in coming. He came to call for me so late, we didn't go on the date. We just went out for ice cream. He liked ice cream and I did too. I never tasted ice cream in Europe; I didn't know what it was like. The first time I had it was here in America.

When did he propose to you?
It was supposed to be the second date, but we didn't do anything, we just went across the street. We sat there in the drug store killing time. We came home a little bit later, the door was closed already - my father used to close it about 9, 10 o'clock. Everyone who was home was upstairs and everyone who was out was out.

We were sitting in the kitchen, and out of the clear sky this guy turns around to me and he proposes! I was stunned. In the first place, I was too young. In the second place, I had two older sisters. In the third place, or maybe in the first place, I knew my mother . . . [makes a gesture?] because no younger sister can get married before the older one is married. That's out. So, I told him that I will think about it, talk about it, and we will see. I gave no answer. And that was it. He wasn't quite ready to get married then, but he was worried. He told me many times he couldn't sleep nights because he was worried I would get away - somebody would grab me off.

He wouldn't let go. He was there every evening. Finally, when I said yes, I would not consider marriage for two years, until I'm 20 or 21. And I told him why. My mother wouldn't have it. I wouldn't do anything my mother wouldn't be happy about. He felt this he can handle, but he couldn't. We were engaged two years.

And your mother still objected?
Very unhappy, Mother. But finally Uncle Phil got after her.

And so she finally relented?
Yes, finally! I was close to 21 when we were married. And by that time Aunt Lena was married. And Grandpa said to her (Rifka) "Look, how do you know that maybe . . . we'll invite a lot of people and maybe she'll be lucky enough to meet somebody at our wedding." He talked her into it. He knew how to handle her. He wrote her a beautiful Yiddish letter. He thanked her for

bringing this wondrous person into his life. I feel so bad that I didn't save that letter. I should have. However, I must have mislaid it somewhere. I couldn't have thrown it away.

It's still around somewhere.
Yeah, I mislaid it.

> *I thought I had found this letter in a box in the Wildwood Avenue attic, written in Yiddish, dated June 22, 1915, two days after the wedding.*

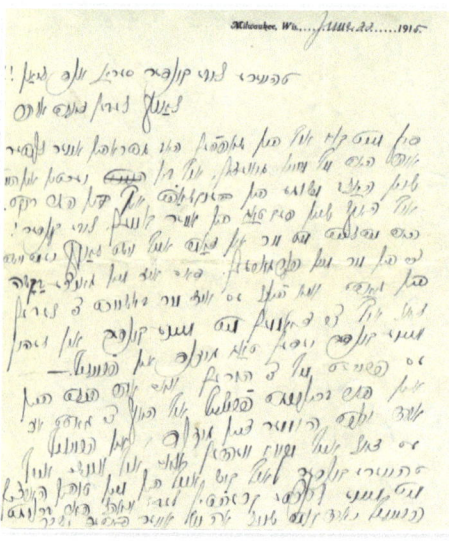

FROM THE IN-LAWS:
After much difficulty in finding someone with knowledge of Yiddish cursive, I finally was able to have it translated, but it is from Rifka and Isaac to Leo and Sarah, most likely in reply to Leo's letter, not the letter Sarah refers to.

My Beloved Children Sarah and Leon,

You should live a long life. I am lost without you today.
I am already half meshugah from longing over you and missing you so much.
I hope the day will come when you will come to me, dear children.
This is my entire request, to be able to be with my children.
I hope to god you will be well. I kiss you with all of my heart and all of my strength.

{Isaac's writing:}

Dear Children,

Have a good mazel, come home for Shabbat, sleep well and in good health.
I kiss you
Your loving father

Mr. and Mrs. I. H. Srulowitz
requests the honor of your presence at the
marriage of their daughter

Sarah
to
Mr. Leo Zucker

on Sunday June twentieth
nineteen hundred and fifteen
at five o'clock p. m.
At the Congregation Anshe Roumania
Eleventh and Sherman Sts.
Milwaukee, Wisconsin

Bride's Residence
628 Walnut St.

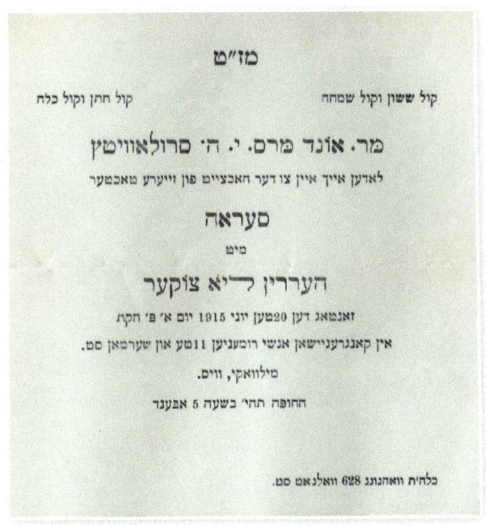

June 20th, 1915: A rare photo of Leo with glasses.

AMERICA

CONGREGATION ANSHE ROMANIA: On the corner of Sherman & 11th St. on Milwaukee's Southside. Originally built by a Presbyterian congregation in the late 19th Century, it was purchased by Romanian Jewish immigrants in 1912.

BEFORE THE INVENTION OF SMILING

Seating a whopping 600 worshippers, the building was remodeled by the congregation in 1922 and torn down along with everything else in Milwaukee, in 1967.

GREAT GRANDFATHER: Rabbi Solomon Scheinfeld married Leo and Sarah. It's unknown whether there were enough family and friends to fill all 600 seats.

SMALL WORLD: With Milwaukee friend John Scheinfeld, and his mom, Audrey. Now a documentary film maker in Los Angeles, I remember him mentioning years ago, that his great grandfather was an Orthodox Rabbi, but I had no clue he had married my grandparents! When I finally realized the connection, all I could think of was… Sheinfeld!?

So Aunt Frieda still wasn't married?
No, but Aunt Frieda became engaged at our wedding. I invited Jack Krasno to be an usher at my wedding. He stood up there with my sister. And when we were on our honeymoon, Aunt Frieda wrote a letter and told us Jack proposed to her and she's engaged to be married! So that's how it happened. And here you all are!

One more thing. So … did you have to shave your head, like you promised?

Oh, (laughs) Well the day of the wedding, I said to her, "Now, Mother, as I promised, I'll shave my head." But she shook her head and said, "Don't worry, you don't have to. This is America."

*   *   *

This ends the transcript of the 1976 interview. For some reason I can't remember, we didn't go on from the 1915 wedding. But the story certainly doesn't end here, and what follows is what I've been able to put together from my own memory of family stories, from photographs, news articles, and some of the 10 Zucker first cousins.

Who needs Grandma, anyway?

PART THREE

BURTON

STARTER HOME: The miserable president Woodrow Wilson was at the end of his first term in 1915 as Sarah and Leo moved into the ground floor of this duplex at 2529 N. 9th St. On the second floor lived Frieda with her husband, Jack Krasno and their son, Sid. My dad, Burton Charles Zucker, was born on July 4th, 1916, during the Battle of The Somme.

PEEPING TOM: Anxious to rise above her immigrant status, Sarah wanted more than anything to show off a first class American home to family and guests. According to Mom, since she wasn't invited into the neighbors homes, she would peek into the next door house to learn the proper way to set a table.

ON THE SPOT: I remembered seeing this picture of Grandma holding my dad on this wall, and was able to locate the house while on a July, 2016 trip to Milwaukee for a high school reunion. I'm standing on the same spot [inset] exactly 100 years later.

NICE STRAW HATS!: Leo pushes the 1916 baby carriage, with Maury, Grandma, Bee and Rifka. She kept it long after its use, surviving in the various attics of the family residences until the Wildood Avenue house was sold in 2002. Today it's owned by someone with enough space for an antique baby carriage.

GOOFY: My Dad at age two. With Sarah, Frieda and first cousin Sid Krasno.

BEFORE THE INVENTION OF SMILING

BRILL "BAR MIZWAH": Aug 24, 1919 - For another ten bucks, you'd think they could afford a photographer who could spell. Shortly after this photo was taken, the brothers and sisters shortened the Srulovitz name to "Surlow." Burt, 3, is in lower left corner, Sarah and Leo, top center and inset. Leo's holding some unknown child. What's known for certain is that everyone in the picture is now dead.

Burton Age Four: If you were a parent in 1920, evidently this is what you wanted your child to look like.

MORE DEAD PEOPLE: Pesach, April 12th 1922: TOP ROW: Sam and Mildred Surlow, Joe and Fanny Brill, Jack snd Frieda Krasno, Phil and Ann Surlow, Harry and Lena Lieberthal, Sarah and Leo. 2nd ROW: Maury, Bee, Martin 'Curly' Brill, Isaac & Rifka, Leonard Brill, BOTTOM ROW: Sid Krasno, Mildred Lieberthal, Burt Zucker, Bernice Lieberthal, Arlene Surlow.

ANOTHER FRONT PORCH: From 8th St. the family moved to 3615 W. Highland Ave. in 1920. My uncle, Bob Zucker, was born December 2nd, 1921.

TOM SAWYER: Dad (right) in the lead role, tricking his pal, "Ben" in a long forgotten mid 1920's school play. An early Zucker stage performance.

HIGHLAND AVE. 1924: Three years later, they posed for this picture on the front steps. Across the street, freight trains rumbled past, around the corner, the Miller Brewery, and right beyond that, the future County Stadium Miller Park, and now American Family Field, home of the Milwaukee Brewers. As on 9th St., the Krasnos occupied the second floor. There was a pool table in the attic. Sid and Burt were best friends, and often would get into some kind of malicious mischief. One family story had them throwing potatoes at cars from the 2nd floor balcony. I suspect there were others, since years later, whenever I'd get in trouble, the outrage would come from Mom. Dad was always somehow strangely silent.

Dad at 10. With Grandma and Uncle Bob, (c. 1926) location unknown.

At some point during this time Leo created his own department store, which he named Daly's, reportedly chosen by looking for American-sounding names in the Milwaukee phone directory.

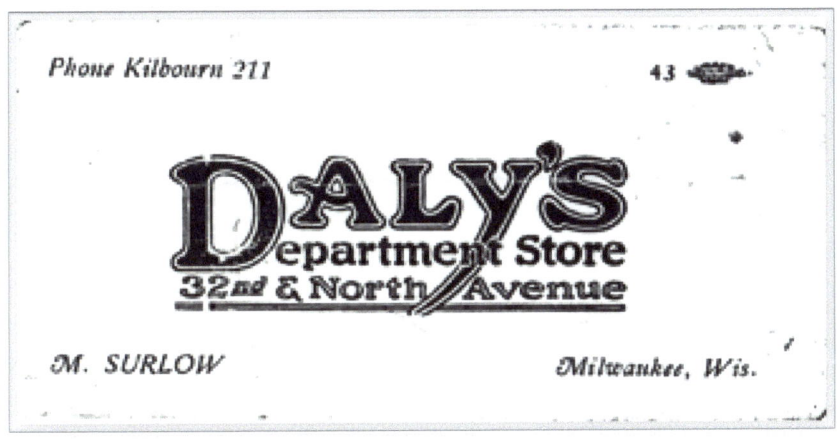

DALY'S DEPARTMENT STORE: Before Uncle Maury started his own store, he worked for Leo at Daly's and carried this card, with the very easy to remember phone number.

According to Uncle Maury, he once talked Leo into letting him order a large quantity of men's shoes which had become available at a very low price. Despite the apparent bargain, Leo was still skeptical and turned the idea down. But Maury was persistent and somehow persuaded Leo to let him order some huge quantity (in today's terminology, a "shitload") of shoes. When, as Leo predicted, they didn't move, Maury was mortified and embarrassed, but remembered Leo said nothing and never mentioned it again.

GOLDMAN'S DEPARTMENT STORE, 2003 Uncle Bob Zucker, pictured here on a tour of Zucker related Milwaukee sites with daughter, Debbie, explained that this store was very much what Daly's would have looked like.

WORTH THE MOVE: Shorewood High School, on W. Capitol Dr. in Shorewood, 1931.

With Burton aged 15 and the promise of better schools, Leo decided to rent a house in the recently (1924) incorporated Milwaukee suburb of Shorewood.

YET ANOTHER DUPLEX: 4425 N Cramer St: From 1931 to summer of 1936, again with the Krasnos occupying the second floor.

BEFORE THE INVENTION OF SMILING

FORMAL PORTRAIT: The family in the Cramer St. living room, minus Leo, most likely the photographer.

SHOREWOOD, 1931: Uncle Bob reading under an oil painting by Milwaukee artist Francesco Spicuzza (1883-1962) whose daughter, Marguerite (Miss Spicuzza) was my 4th grade art teacher.

LOS ANGELES 2022: The Spicuzza, today, in my living room. reframed, and restored by Milwaukee art dealer, and former Shorewood High School student, David Barnett.

JIM ZUCKER: Born March 23, 1929.

1999: The three brothers. Jim, Bob, Burt.

"WE'RE FINISHED!"

Leo, like many other Americans in the 1920's, had invested heavily in the stock market, much of his purchases made "on margin," borrowing in hopes of making future profits. But the 1929 Wall Street crash put an end to the plan and Leo found himself struggling to keep Daly's Department Store. Finally, one morning at breakfast in 1932, according to Dad, Leo answered a phone call, listened for a moment, nodded, hung up, turned to Grandma and said, simply, "We're finished."

> " What a scary moment that must have been for Burt to hear that exchange as a teen. I don't think my dad remembered that specific comment, but he did tell me about sensing his parents' fears and worries. Dad was only about nine or ten in 1929, but he was 14 in 1932 when they drove to Canada, probably to get a loan from the Lax family in Hamilton, Ontario. Dad remembered that trip clearly. It seems to me that Grandpa Leo took a lot of big risks, and maybe was used to being overextended. If so, that would shed light on some of my dad's more conservative, second-generation earning and spending habits. Unlike his Dad, my Dad wasn't a new immigrant, without formal education.
>
> - Debbie Zucker "

MAX LAX: Wife was named Goldie Lax (You couldn't make this up.) then divorced her, who then became known as Ex-Lax. (*That's* made up.)

Leo was forced to sell Daly's Department Store but evidently wasn't completely broke, since according to Debbie, he bought a brand new car, and the family set out for Canada (16 year old Burton doing much of the driving) to visit Uncle Max Lax, who was in the scrap iron business in Hamilton,

OCTOBER 1959: Hamilton, Ontario. L to R: Max, Dad, Morris Karn, Esther Lax.

> "Max and Goldie Lax lived in Hamilton, Ontario. Our family visited them once, sometime in the 70's maybe, at Max's scrap-metal yard there. Max was a friendly man. I remember he was working, in overalls, along with everyone else in the scrapyard. He must have been both successful and generous in that he was able to loan Leo enough to basically start over. Our family always loved that Max's wife was named Goldie Lax! For real!
> - Debbie Zucker"

Once there, Leo asked Max to lend him enough money to start a chain of "dollar dress stores", a concept gaining popularity in many cities during the Depression. He chose the name "Hollywood Shops." Eventually there were 17 of them. An instant success, Leo was able to buy a building in downtown Milwaukee on Plankington Ave, to manufacture the dresses and aprons to be sold in the stores, under the name: "Supreme Dress Co."

HOLLYWOOD SHOPS: This location was at the corner of 5th and National on Milwaukee's South side. When Dad later joined the business, he asked Leo to let him try renting the vacant office space on the 2nd and 3rd floors, which he did, much to his father's delight. Becoming far more interested in this than the dreary retail clothing business, Dad eventually found success and happiness in commercial real estate.

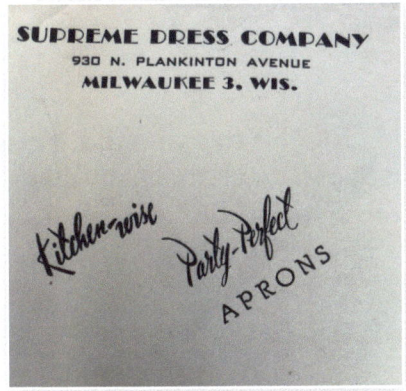

> Grandma often filled in at the stores, and was an excellent salesperson. When I was 13, I worked during the summer, waiting on women who were shopping for dresses, underwear, etc. Because I was so young, Grandma occasionally gave me some advice so I wouldn't come across as a total neophyte. She would tell me, 'when a customer is trying on clothing and they ask for your opinion, don't lie and tell them they look great if they don't. Instead, you can soften the truth, but always be positive, friendly…and smile. She also stressed the importance of saying 'hello' to each customer who came in. She said, "even if you're busy with another customer, always welcome them into the store."
> - Susan Zucker Breslau

By 1935, Leo was doing well enough to be able to build a new house, and bought property in Shorewood, the first suburb north of Milwaukee. This time there was to be no duplex, the Krasnos were on their own. They built a house two blocks away, on Ardmore Ave.

THE MILWAUKEE JOURNAL

New Home in Shorewood

ONE of the largest homes to be built in Shorewood in several years is this Lannon stone English style home under construction on N. Wildwood av., Palo Alto subdivision. It has four bedrooms and three baths on the second floor and has an air conditioning heating plant. It was designed and built by William F. Thalman, Inc.

DOUBLE LOT: Not content with a duplex or even a single lot, Leo bought two, and Sarah hired architect builder William Thalman to build her dream house, an English style Cotswold, built of Wisconsin Lannon Stone. Often, Sarah would hand pick the stones for the masons, leaving the rust colored ones for the back of the house, where they can still be seen today.

UNDER CONSTRUCTION: Wildwood Avenue, 1935. Leo had the wonderful idea of buying the three adjacent lots for Burt, Bob and Jim so they could all live on the same block, together, next to each other, forever,. Fortunately, Grandma was able to talk him out of it.

KELMSCOTT MANOR, West Oxfordshire England: Sarah became enthralled with the 16th century Cotswold style in southern England, although she had never been there, and the internet was still 60 years away. A far cry from any architecture she may have remembered in late 19th century Austria-Hungary, in her mind it was the embodiment of a dream home.

WILDWOOD AVE: Shorewood, Wisconsin, 1936. Final construction cost: $18,000, barely enough to cover my last year's kitchen remodel.

MRS. LEO ZUCKER, 1941: New Address.

VAL KILMER and GIRLFRIEND, 1984: On the set of "Top Secret!" Pinewood Studios, London, the prisoner number "4395" on his shirt. Cher kept telling him what a stupid movie it was and how it would flop at the box office. Never mind she was right, it was just annoying.

1938: Burt's a sophomore at the University of Wisconsin-Madison, Bob at Shorewood High School, Jim at Lake bluff Elementary. Second row: Frieda, Sarah, Rifka, Fanny, Bee. Lena in 3rd row.

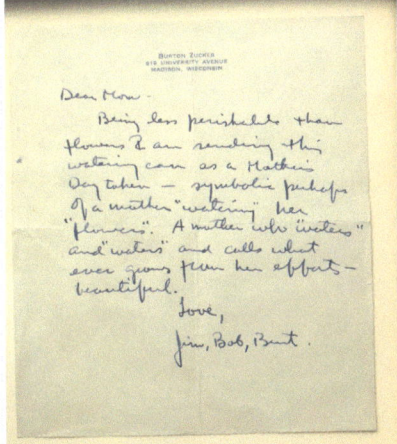
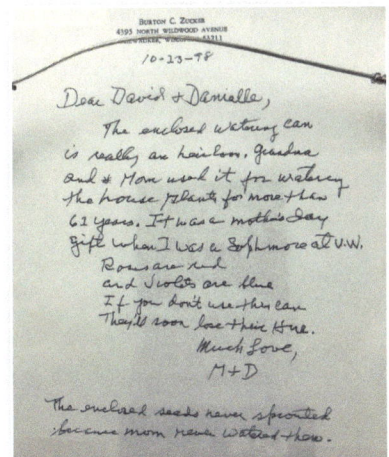

MOTHER'S DAY: On May 8th, 1938, the brothers presented a copper watering can to Sarah. It was used in the Wildwood house for many years but I hadn't realized its history until Dad sent it to me with the attached explanation in 1998. Then I discovered the original note in Mom and Dad's papers in 2008.

Dear Mom,

Being less perishable than flowers I am sending this watering can as a Mother's Day token - symbolic perhaps of a mother "watering" her "flowers" A mother who "waters" and 'waters" and calls whatever grows from her efforts - beautiful.

Love,
Jim, Bob, Burt

BEFORE THE INVENTION OF SMILING

BEING LESS PERISHABLE: On display today on my bookshelf.

WILDWOOD 1941: The watering can for 60 years resided on this beautiful knotty pine counter. Grandma, although from East Bumble Turd, Hungary, somehow had acquired a wonderful design sense and a reverence for the traditional. But sometime deep in the 1970's, Mom came under the spell of an evil decorator and all the woodwork was painted over...Ugh. In this photo, the watering can (circled) is shown on the formerly beautiful knotty pine counter.

WILDWOOD 1940: On the Congress St. side. With Sarah's sister, Lena Lieberthal, and her daughters Bernice and Mildred, and son Alan.

WEDDING ANNIVERSARY: Sunday, June 23rd, 1940. Burt had finished his senior year at the University off Wisconsin- Madison. Grandma and Grandpa celebrated their 25th anniversary. These frames were taken from 16mm color film of the Wildwood Ave. party.

BEFORE THE INVENTION OF SMILING

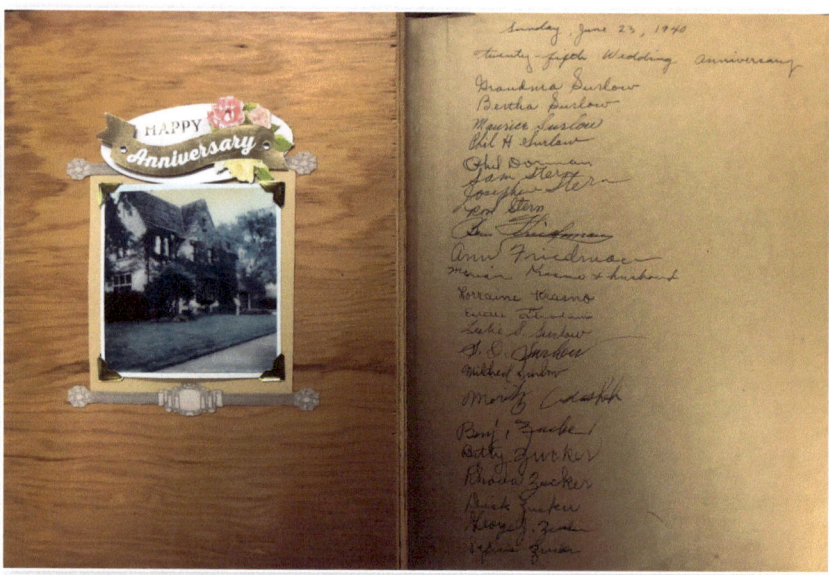

GUESTBOOK: 25th Wedding Anniversary, 1940.

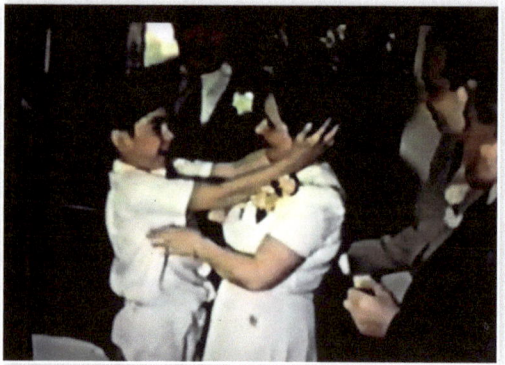

B'NAI B'RITH HILLEL FOUNDATION
AT THE UNIVERSITY OF WISCONSIN
508 State Street   Madison, Wisconsin

RABBI MAX KADUSHIN, D.H.L.
　Director
BURTON ZUCKER
　Student Director

HILLEL FOUNDATION: Back in Madison, as massive German air raids began in 1940's London, Dad (far right, above left photo) began his duties as Student Director of the UW Hillel Foundation. Rabbi Max Kadushin (below) was the Rabbi-Director. Above right photo - Dad with Hillel students.

BEFORE THE INVENTION OF SMILING

UNIVERSITY OF WISCONSIN - MADISON ARMORY & GYMNASIUM: Commonly known as "The Red Gym," located on the shore of Lake Mendota, it opened in 1894, right after Sarah's birth. Just a scant 72 years later, I endured gym classes here as a UW Freshman, doing laps in a long since removed swimming pool.

LOVE AT FIRST SIGHT: Here, at the top of the second floor stairs of the red gym, in January of 1941, during a Hillel Foundation dance, Dad met 19-year-old Brooklyn College graduate, Charlotte Lefstein. She had just arrived in Madison to begin graduate school in Speech. They had corresponded briefly in the previous month concerning Hillel, but after chatting for a few moments, Dad turned to his friend, fellow Milwaukee native Phil Lerman, and said, "I'll be right back. Take care of my girl."

BEFORE THE INVENTION OF SMILING

WHEN PEOPLE DANCED: Mom and Dad are at the far left, just out of frame.

FIRST DATE: Dad took Mom to the Wisconsin Student Union, on the shore of lake Mendota. They had dessert in the Paul Bunyan Room, known for its' WPA murals of the legendary Wisconsin super hero. For years afterward, they would commemorate the event by having "Peach Pie and Milk."

1990: Back for a visit to Madison, they sat in the same booth. Nothing much had changed from 1941 except Peach Pie and milk was no longer available.

SCHOOL PLAY: Charlotte, a natural actress, soon began performing in UW Players dramas at the Wisconsin Union.

MARCH 1941: Snow still visible on the ground, Charlotte is enthralled with Dad's sense of humor.

Or was she acting?

COZY: Snow longer visible, and it's definitely getting warmer.

DO I HAVE TO MARRY HER?: By late May, Dad's mind was set on bringing his new girl — and the laundry — home.

B'NAI B'RITH HILLEL FOUNDATION
AT THE UNIVERSITY OF WISCONSIN
508 State Street   Madison, Wisconsin

RABBI MAX KADUSHIN, D.H.L.
Director

BURTON ZUCKER
Student Director

B'NAI B'RITH MAINTAINS
FOUNDATIONS AT
University of Illinois
University of Wisconsin
Ohio State University
University of Michigan
University of California
Cornell University
University of Texas
University of Alabama
Pennsylvania State College
Indiana University
University of Chicago
Northwestern University
University of North Carolina
University of Florida
University of Georgia
University of Iowa
University of Maryland
University of Minnesota
Texas A. & M. College
University of Virginia
Brooklyn College
Queen's University (Canada)
University of Washington

B'NAI B'RITH MAINTAINS
COUNSELORS AT
Alabama Polytechnic
University of Arizona
Bucknell University
Duke University
Florida College for Women
Franklin & Marshall College
Iowa State College
Ithaca College
University of Kentucky
Lafayette College
Lehigh University
Massachusetts State College
University of Miami (Fla)
Miami University (Ohio)
Michigan State College
Michigan State Normal
Mississippi State College
University of Mississippi
Moravian College
Muhlenberg College
University of Missouri
University of Nebraska
University of New Hampshire
Ohio University
University of Oregon
Purdue University
Rutgers University
Smith College
Transylvania College
University of South Carolina
University of Utah
University of West Virginia

Sunday

Dear Mom,

    Just talked with Bob and am going to go out to the dorms to have supper with him this evening. We'll eat in the Pine Room. He's studying for his exams..has the first one on Wednesday. Had Jean out for supper the other night. We ate on the Union terrace and I think she liked it good. The more I see of Jeanie the more I like her.

    I forgot completely about my laundry this week and luckily Phil's brother was in town today to take it in for me.

    Has anything been done about the father's day gift for Pop? Bob and I are still with you on the radio proposition which I think is a good idea. Let me know what's up. Kadushin told me that he met Pop on the train and that they rode to Milwaukee together or something.

    I'm pretty well cleaned up with all my work and probably will be able to go into Milwaukee with Bob next Sunday. At any rate I'll send all my stuff in with Bob.

    We're getting a complete remodeling job here at the foundation and we're all involved in plans for the work now.

    What do you say to bringing my girl Charlotte in to Milwaukee for a visit. Could she stay with us? Or do I have to marry her first? Syd and Dave may take a jaunt in too.

    Once again being sort of fed up with Madison I'm looking foreward to being at home. I really want to work hard this summer. I need the dicipline and besides I'm getting to fat around the mid section.

    I guess thats all now,

            Love to all,

A National Organization Devoted to Cultural, Religious and Social Work Among Jewish Students in American Universities

MEETING CHARLOTTE: Mom seems to have been a hit, at least with Grandma. It's unknown what the exact sleeping arrangements were.

MATCH MADE IN HEAVEN: In reality, everyone loved Mom, but for Grandma, Charlotte was the daughter she never had. Mom, who had lost her own mother, (also named Sarah) just three years before to Tuberculosis, gained a mentor, teacher, confidant, and mom in her future mother-in-law.

PROPOSAL: In early September, Charlotte, then back in New York, got a call from Burt, "How about coming to Milwaukee in two weeks to get married?" The urgency, was in part due to the impending military draft, and perhaps a need to solve the limited bedroom dilemma. In preparation for the upcoming nuptials, Burt mailed Charlotte a one way train ticket and a sex manual. It was 1941.

WEDDING: In an astonishingly short time, Grandma was able to pull together the wedding, held in the Wildwood living room on September 19. Max Kadushin, of the Hillel Foundation, presided. Mom descended the entry hall steps to walk down the aisle, past a guy so overcome by emotion, he forgot to take off his hat.

PROUD MOM: Sarah left no doubt as to how she felt about her first born's marriage, setting a new world record for Mothers of Grooms Photographed Beaming.

DECEMBER 7: Three months later, the Japanese attacked Pearl Harbor and Dad was drafted into the US Army Air Force.

"12 O'CLOCK HIGH": His job was briefing pilots before their bombing missions, just like James Stewart and Spencer Tracy did — except in Orlando Florida on training missions. Eventually he made Tech. Sergeant, my elementary school classmates heard the version where he fought in the Battle of Central Florida.

B-24: Dad, on far left, inspects one of those really cool planes.

Endless Marching: Dad, 23rd from far left.

HOME ON FURLOUGH: 1942, the family in the Wildwood living room. The lamp and table on the far left is now in my upstairs hall, with the accompanying photo nearby.

BOOK TABLE: (Left) Once Aunt Bee and Uncle Maury's, unique book table, in the 1930's it was a reproduction of a 19th century antique, but now an antique in its own right. There was always a bowl on top of it, filled with M&M's. On Fall Sundays, it would empty while Jerry and I, with Zucker first cousins Michael and Bill, watched Green Bay Packer games (in color!) with Uncle Maury.

THE WAR YEARS: Mom and Dad were able to live together through most of the war in a cottage on the base. Grandma and Grandpa came for at least one visit. Mom and Dad went back for a visit in the 90's, but everything was gone.

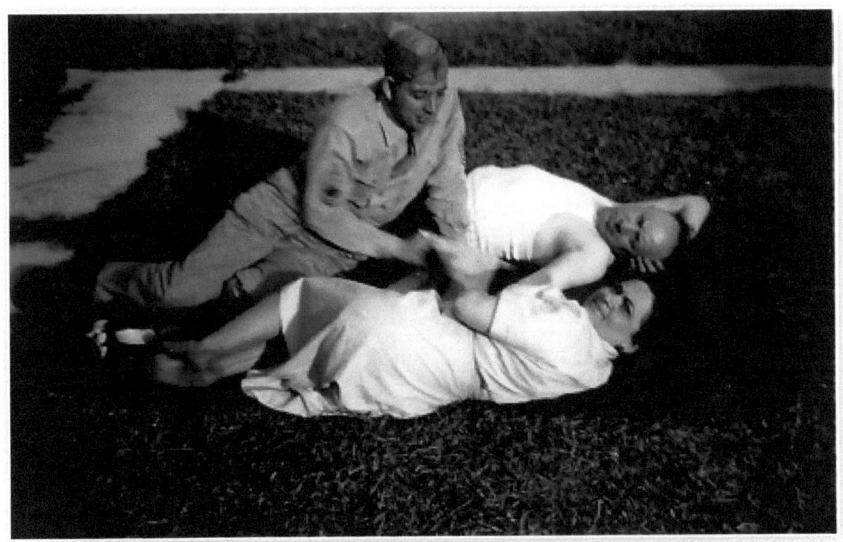

BEFORE THE INVENTION OF SMILING

> Mom told the story of how she and Dad enjoyed evening walks around the base, talking at length. Invariably, the subject would turn to the future. And Mom would ask, "Tell me about the Rabbits," a reference to the recent 1937 John Steinbeck novel "Of Mice and Men." And Dad would describe the home they would live in, three kids, a garden, everything that awaited them after the war. She loved hearing that, and felt much better, until she asked him the next time.
> - Jerry Zucker

LAKE DOT: March 1943

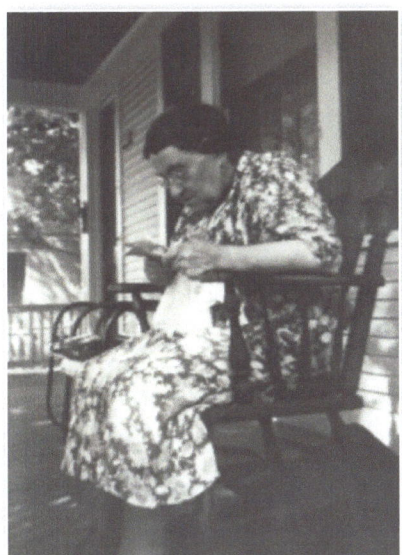

1943: The last photo of Rifka, reading, I'd like to think, a letter from her grandson, although it would have had to be translated into Yiddish, since she never learned English.

OBITUARY

MRS. RIFKA SURLOW

Funeral services were held at the Goodman and Sons chapel, 1701 W. Walnut street, for Mrs. Rifka Surlow, 68, who died last week at her home, 2348 N. Forty-eighth street.

Born in Hungary, Mrs. Surlow came to Milwaukee 34 years ago. She was a member of the Eva Sisters of Congregation Beth Israel, the Milwaukee Jewish Children's home and the Home for Aged Jews.

Survivors are three sons, Philip, Samuel D., and Maurice; five daughters, Mrs. Fannie Brill, Mrs. Lena Lieberthal, Mrs. J. E. Krasno, Mrs. Leo Zucker and Bertha Surlow, and four brothers, Max Stern of Milwaukee, Joseph, Jacob and Isidore Stern, all of Kenosha.

Burial took place in Second Home cemetery.

FAKE NEWS: Even in 1943. (Rifka was 86, not 68.)

ORANGES: Grandpa had his pick, and according to Uncle Jim, amazed that these things actually grew on trees.

CLOSE CALL: In July of 1945, Dad was shipped to Fort Collins, Colorado, and then on to Oakland, California where he was to be transported with hundreds of thousands of other soldiers for the impending invasion of Japan. They were marching down to the dock when the ship's boiler blew up. Soon after, the war ended with the atomic bombing of Hiroshima and Nagasaki, and Mom and Dad came home, to live at Wildwood. He, along with Uncle Bob and later, Uncle Jim, went to work for Leo in the retail and manufacturing dress business.

WHEN SHE ACTUALLY BECAME "GRANDMA": Susan was born May 30, 1946, signaling the official start of the Baby Boom.

Below: The new Grandpa, facing the wonderful Knotty Pine Cabinetry, which was to have 30 more years of being wonderful.

PART FOUR

DAVID

Photograph courtesy of the Milwaukee County Historical Society, *1947 Milwaukee Blizzard*

"BLIZZARD OF '47": January 30, 1947. The biggest blizzard in all of Milwaukee's recorded history stopped the city cold, more than 18 inches of snow falling in 3 days, with wind gusts up to 60 MPH. Before television was widely available and limited radio, residents were forced to pass the time creating their own entertainment.

SURPRISING COINCIDENCE: I was born nine months later, Oct. 16, 1947.

WHITEFISH BAY: Mom and Dad bought a house in the suburb north of Shorewood for $11,500, approximately what it would cost today to restore the Knotty Pine cabinetry. Even at that price, Dad told me Grandpa thought he paid too much for it.

MISSED OPPORTUNITY: The house, at 4781 N. Diversey Boulevard was only one street west of *Hollywood* Ave. I couldn't believe we missed it by one street!

JERRY: Born March 11, 1950. Now officially The Zucker Brothers. And Sister.

GRANDMA & GRANDPA: Grandma always described Grandpa in the most glowing terms, once adding: "He worshipped the ground I walked on." This is what I always felt was the key ingredient for a successful marriage. I've yet to find anyone who'll worship me like *that*.

Obituaries

Leo Zucker

Services were held at the Goodman funeral home for Leo Zucker, 61, of 3495 N. Wildwood ave., who died suddenly Monday, June 18.

Mr. Zucker, a native of Russia, came to Milwaukee in 1907. He was president of the Supreme Dress Co. He was a charter member of Congregation Beth El, and a member of the Home for Aged Jews, of B'nai B'rith, of Temple Emanu-El B'ne Jeshurrun, of the Zionist Organization of America, and of the Elks club.

Survivors are his wife, Sarah; three sons, James, Robert and Burton; a brother, Milton; two sisters, Esther Zucker and Mrs. Ben Zucker, and four grandchildren, all of Milwaukee.

Burial was in Second Home cemetery.

LEO ZUCKER 1891 - 1952: On a Monday in June, Leo, age 61, suffered a massive heart attack at his desk in the Supreme Dress Company offices on Plankington Ave. Dad phoned the next door neighbor, Shirley Rumack, first, so she could be with Mom when she heard the news. He thought of stuff like that. When next we came to visit Grandma, Mom and Dad made sure that I understood not to mention Grandpa. Of course as soon as we walked in the door, my first words were, "Where's Grandpa?" Grandma had to excuse herself.

NICE WALLPAPER: 1953, (rare photo includes Dad) but what makes me wince is the wonderful old radio on the shelf that no one thought to save. Most likely it's the radio suggested to Bob as a potential Father's Day gift in Burt's 1941 letter (p. 153) - it was later given back to Burt. Damn!

GREEN BAY: Four years before the arrival of Vince Lombardi, with the Packers preparing for yet another miserable season, Grandma's youngest, Jim, married Eve Joan Peal, a native of Green Bay. Her father, Lew Peal, had been a pal of Curly Lambeau and hung out with other Packers founders in the 1920's, but I had no idea how really cool this was until much later. Uncle Bob and Aunt Ecy are at right with their daughter, Nancy, now of Madison and a grandma herself.

> In 1918, my father, Lew Peal, was the manager of a ladies dress shop in Green Bay, catering to large women. One of his young salesgirls, Margurite Van Kessel, was dating a local factory worker named Curly Lambeau. Every day at 3pm, when his shift ended, Curly would appear at the dress shop to hang out with Marguerite. At first, Dad was annoyed, but eventually he asked Curly to walk to the railroad station to pick up the dresses that were sent from Chicago each day. Before long, he and Curly became best friends, even going on golf outings together. On one of these, Curly mentioned an idea he had for starting a football team, but he lacked the money. Lew suggested he approach his boss at the Indian Packing Co. and offer to name the team after the business for publicity. Curly took him up on it and The Green Bay Packers were born. Dad sat on his board of directors for many years. After a stint on a destroyer with the Sixth Fleet in the Mediterranean, I became Vince Lombardi's travel agent and handled all the Packers travel for 19 years which included Super Bowls I and II.
> - Dick Peal

Dick Peal with a travel agency client.*

Dick Peal: "Dad snapped this 1931 photo of Curly and Marguerite, beer toasting my mom, Ida, on the upcoming birth of my sister, Eve Joan. Mom is in the lower right corner in an early attempt at a photo bomb."

2023: The author, with daughter, Sarah at the Lew Peal-inspired Lambeau Field.

* Dick Peal's agency client: Bart Starr, Hall of Famer and MVP of Superbowls I & II.

FIRST STAGE PERFORMANCE: Grandpa didn't ask for much, but according to Grandma, he insisted on *high ceilings*. The architect, William Thalman complied by designing a sunken living room. The Zucker Brothers immediately saw it for what it was, a stage! The arch offered a natural proscenium. On a typical Hanukah the relatives were the captive audience, treated to a singing and comedy show. Whatever the dialogue was for this no doubt hilarious sketch is lost to history.

17 YEARS LATER: The Zucker Brothers onstage once again, performing in their comedy revue, Kentucky Fried Theater on the University of Wisconsin - Madison campus.

BEFORE THE INVENTION OF SMILING

BACK TO 1954: The only known photograph of all the Surlow siblings together. Although it's unclear what occasion could have been important enough to garner the attendance of all eight, we can be certain it involved eating.

NEW DIGS: In September of 1955, our family moved into the Wildwood Ave. house, Grandma moved to an apartment, and I began the third grade at Lake Bluff School, a short bike ride away.

LAKE BLUFF SCHOOL: Sometime during the 4th grade I got the idea of writing my own comic books. Most were entitled: "George & Tiny."

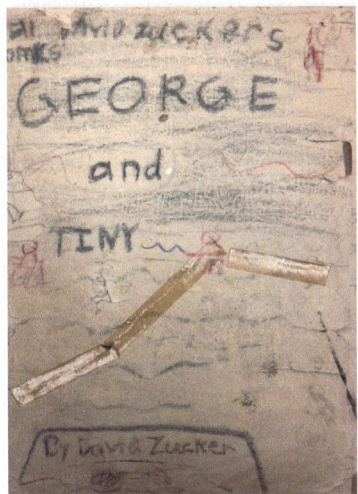
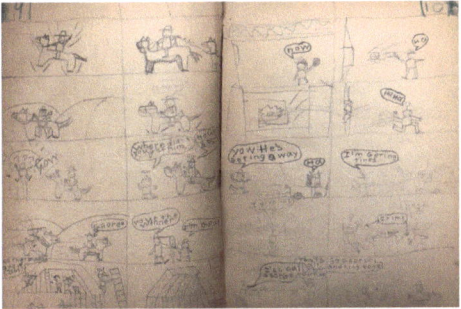

GEORGE & TINY: They proved to be so popular among my classmates, I had to have them "mimeographed" and distributed throughout the school. It soon attracted the attention of the art teacher, Miss Spicuzza, who promptly yanked me out of class for a trip to the principal's office.

MISS SPICUZZA: I was relieved to discover she loved my comic books and thought them so unusual that the principal needed to see them. She lived into her 90's and died in 2010. I wish now I had gone to visit.

ROCK STAR: Having formed my own rock band as a Shorewood High School freshman, our group, "The Chevelles" (all the good cars were taken) played at school dances, Bar Mitzvahs, and fraternity parties as far away as Madison and Chicago. When bookings were scarce, we'd rent a hall on our own and throw a dance. It was at one of these events, in June of 1964 in Milwaukee's Lincoln Park, that Mom brought Grandma. For the first time, she saw, and heard, her grandson rocking out to covers of Chuck Berry, The Beatles, Bo Diddley, and more. Her reaction: "The girls aren't wearing bras." To this day I don't understand what she was talking about..

"WHAT? I HAVE NO MEMORY OF THAT." Outside her Kensington Blvd. apartment in Shorewood. Grandma had opposed this large development when construction started in the 1940's, but years later, she admitted there were certain advantages.

RIFKA: Hanukah, 1941

ZUCKER TRADITION: Hanukah, 1966. Grandma, as Rifka had done before *her*, Yehudas before her, and (according to Dad) Adam & Eve Zucker, handing out Hanukah "Gelt" (coins) to all ten grandkids.

75th BIRTHDAY BASH: The Pioneer Inn, Oshkosh, August 25th, 1968.

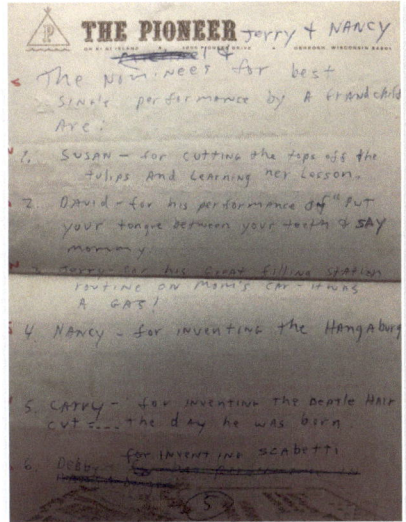 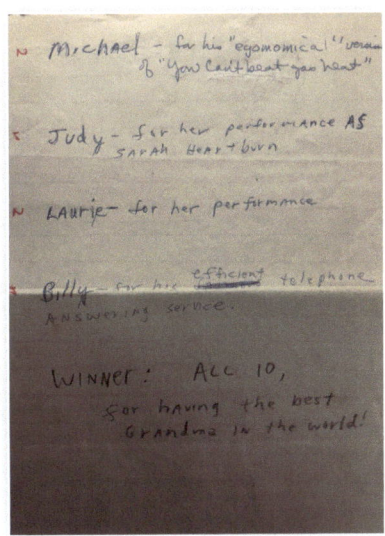

THE GRAMMYS: For the evening's entertainment, Jerry and I wrote, and all the cousins performed, an awards show parody, "The Grammy Awards," complete with the usual chuckle-worthy family stories. I remember having to rush through the final 15 minutes, since Grandma was struggling to keep awake, much like modern day awards show audiences.

"RALLY AT THE MALL! MARCH TO THE CAPITOL!": Back at the University of Wisconsin-Madison (another Zucker tradition) for the Fall semester, we discovered the administration was, for the first time, issuing photo I.D.'s. Everyone was outraged, convinced the purpose was to identify us in anti-war riots. Dozens of my classmates declared with solemn bravado that they would refuse to cooperate. But when the time came, they all caved — except for me.

NOT COMPLETELY THOUGHT OUT: With a ridiculously bad accent, I talked the photographer into taking this picture., but what I didn't figure on was that I had to dress up all over again two weeks later to pick it up.

SENIOR CLASS PRESIDENT:
As with everything else, I just figured out how to do this. With Jerry as my campaign manager, I won by 5 votes.

1971: The Milwaukee wedding reception of my sister and Bill Breslau, Grandma on my arm. Fortunately, I was comfortable enough in the room to be able to walk around with my eyes closed.

BILL BRESLAU: From Vernon, Conn. The Zuckers took an immediate liking to Bill, except for his being a Republican. Thirty years later I realized he was perfect.

With some borrowed videotape equipment, Jim Abrahams, Jerry and I did a video spoofing the wedding, showing it at the rehearsal dinner. As it turned out, a big hit with all the out of town guests - our first effort as a team.

KENTUCKY FRIED: Encouraged by the family reaction, a few months later, combining video material with live sketches, we were able to open The Kentucky Fried Theater, in the former storage room of a Madison bookstore.

JUNE 1, 1972: The Madison KFT was an instant hit, but we needed to be "discovered" - and be able to charge more than a dollar admission. So the ZAZ team left Milwaukee for Los Angeles. Instead of the Prinz Friedrich Wilhelm, we had a U-Haul truck. The six day drive was a fraction of Grandma's two month long 1909 journey, but for us, it was no less of an adventure.

WEST PICO BLVD. LOS ANGELES: As the Srulovitz family had done 63 years earlier, we set up our retail (theater) business, opened the doors, and lived above the store.

BEFORE THE INVENTION OF SMILING

FAMILY BUSINESS: In March of 1973, Aunt Bee and Uncle Maury flew out to to Los Angeles to see the show and posed for this photo with us in the green room. By this time, the cast included our second cousin Mallory Sandler, granddaughter of Uncle Phil. Also attending that night was cousin "Aunt" Shirley Brody, daughter of Uncle Sam, and her husband, Dr. Jack Brody, who was instrumental in getting us the theater building on Pico.

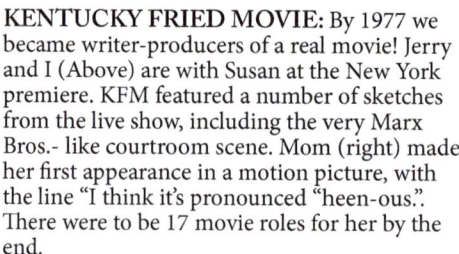

KENTUCKY FRIED MOVIE: By 1977 we became writer-producers of a real movie! Jerry and I (Above) are with Susan at the New York premiere. KFM featured a number of sketches from the live show, including the very Marx Bros.- like courtroom scene. Mom (right) made her first appearance in a motion picture, with the line "I think it's pronounced "heen-ous.". There were to be 17 movie roles for her by the end.

CHARLOTTE ZUCKER FILM HIGHLIGHTS

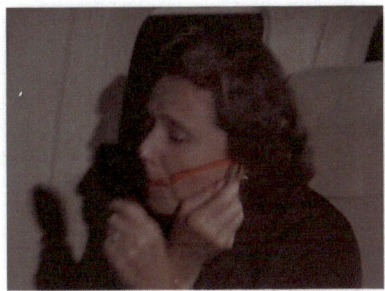

AIRPLANE! (1980): Make up Lady - Leslie Nielsen

GHOST (1990): Bank Officer - Patrick Swayze, Whoopi Goldberg

NAKED GUN (1988) : "I must kill Papshmir!"

MY BOSS'S DAUGHTER (2003): Ashton Kutcher

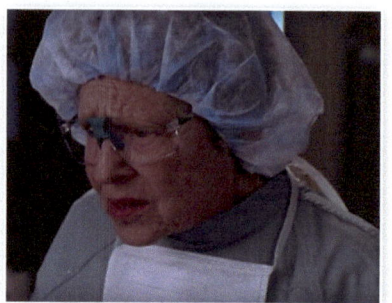

BASEketball (1998): Recovery nurse - Trey Parker, Matt Stone

RAUNCHY: Mom had no problem with the "R"rated humor of KFM and was excited to have been in the courtroom scene. When friends complimented her about her sons' having made a movie, she would thank them and say "And you know, I'm in it!" Then of course the next question was always, "Which part?" and she would reply, "The shower scene!"

FAMILY DEBATE: We were horrified at the thought of Grandma, Aunt Bee and Uncle Maury seeing the raunchy KFM. Dad thought we just had to "face it and let 'em see it." But Jerry, Mom and I decided to show them a specially edited version at home.. Even so, it wasn't cleaned up entirely. At one point, a character simply uttered the word "Shit!" Grandma turned to Mom and shrugged "Just like that!"

THE BEST LAID PLANS: The scheme backfired. The three went to the Fox Bay Theater, together, paid their admission and saw the complete movie, apparently wanting to see the boys' names on the big screen. They certainly saw that, and a lot more. We never heard what the reaction was. I think that in the grand Zucker family tradition, they were proud of us making a success in the movie business, but dismayed that it was in porn.

AIRPLANE!: In the two years after Kentucky Fried Movie, Jerry, Jim and I concentrated on rewriting our 1975 "Airplane!" script, but were unable to find backing until Michael Eisner brought us to Paramount after we were turned down at every other Hollywood studio. Our debt to Eisner is incalculable. Turns out there are actually some genius studio execs.

RED CARPET: By 1980, a week prior to the national release, Mom, Dad and Louise (Abrahams) Yaffe, invited 600 friends and relatives to Whitefish Bay's Fox Bay Theater for what became the *real* premiere of the PG-rated "Airplane!" Aunt Bee and Uncle Maury laughed throughout, enjoying it thoroughly, as did the entire audience. Grandma, having declined considerably in three years, was more impressed with "all the nice colors."

It was an amazing night, a remarkable homecoming. We did a Q&A onstage after the end credits. For me, there was never a moment equal to this one before or since.

"Airplane!" ushered in a new brand of comedy, creating an entire genre, which eventually ended up making close to a billion dollars for the studios. Since Paramount couldn't hide it fast enough, we were able to make a nice living. I was sure we owed a lot of it to that unique brand of Milwaukee humor. I

remember once telling a reporter: "There were half a dozen guys in my high school funnier than I was. They were just able to find jobs."

FAMILY TRADITION: What is it with the Zuckers and bowties? **Above:** With Grandpa and Dad, 1951.

With Jerry, 1980, and **bottom:** my son Charles, at his prom, 2017. Painfully shy, he was desperate to blend in.

SEPTEMBER 28, 1980: Cousin Nancy Zucker married Mike Burns at Bob and Ecy's home in Fox Point. A year later, Aunt Bee, 81, was diagnosed with lung cancer, and died November 11th, 1981. Uncle Maury lived until age 99.

GREAT GRANDCHILDREN: I wish Grandma could've met my own children, but she had the next best thing: Susan's kids Ben and Jeremy.

THE HOME: Grandma continued to decline after 1981 until early in February Dad was awakened by a 2AM phone call. It was a captain George Silverwood of the Shorewood Police Department who told him an elderly woman was found wandering around the frozen streets in her nightgown. "We think it's your mother." It was. And time for Burt, Bob and Jim to move her to the much safer Milwaukee Jewish Home on Prospect Ave. It had been built on the former site of several of those 1890's "castles" that Grandma had loved so much.

"Mike and I visited Grandma in 1984, shortly after Emily was born. A number of family members were there also, I think my folks, Jim and Eve Joan and maybe Burt and Charlotte, too. Emily was crying, and making a bit of a fuss, and suddenly Grandma says out of the blue: 'Baby!' Then, as if that opened the floodgates, she locks eyes with the only non-Zucker there, Mike, and says: 'Get me out of here! Let me live in your garage!' As though her own family had condemned her to live in this state. All I could think of was that if she had ever actually seen Mike's garage, she would have been a lot less enthusiastic."
- Nancy Zucker

NON SPEAKING ROLE: By 1983, Grandma was in a wheelchair, deep in dementia, able to speak only an occasional word.

GOODBYE: The last time I saw Grandma was in July of 1984, right after "Top Secret!" had opened to mixed reviews and disappointing box office. Although the movie was to gain future legendary cult status around the world (like all my flops, ahead of its time) that week I was devastated. Jerry headed for our ranch in Ojai, and I flew to Milwaukee to hang out with friends there and forget about Hollywood. Naturally, I went with Mom and Dad to the Jewish Home. There, Grandma sat, curled up in a wheelchair. It had been a long time since she had said even a word, but we engaged in a chatty, one way conversation, just to hear the sound of our own voices. Out of talk about the hot weather, I casually remarked, "Our movie, Top Secret! just came out…and it bombed!"

Grandma burst out laughing.

Sarah Zucker 1893 - 1985

PART FIVE

CHARLES & SARAH

Dorothy Parker was one the greatest American wits of the twentieth century. She was among my first literary heroes, along with George S. Kaufman and Groucho Marx. Like them, she was certainly drawn to the money offered by the film industry, and spent a number of years in Hollywood, writing screenplays and making more money than she could ever hope to earn with her stories, reviews and poems. So it was that she found herself at MGM, writing a routine biopic to fill the release schedule for the notorious mogul, Sam Goldwyn. Hunched over her typewriter the morning after Goldwyn read her script, she was interrupted by shouting: "Happy Endings! I need *HAPPY... ENDINGS!*" It was Goldwyn who had stormed into her office, waving the script.

Unperturbed, she turned to face him:
"I know this will come as a shock to you, Mr. Goldwyn, but in all of history, which has held billions and billions of people… not a single one ever had a happy ending."

HAPPY ENDING: Charles and Sarah Zucker, at the 2008 funeral of either Mom or Dad, I don't recall. The corollary to Dorthy Parker's words is reflected on their innocent faces. Life goes on. I regret my kids never got to meet their great Grandmother, but they'll meet her through this book, which is why I wrote it.

David Zucker, Los Angeles, 2022

*   *   *

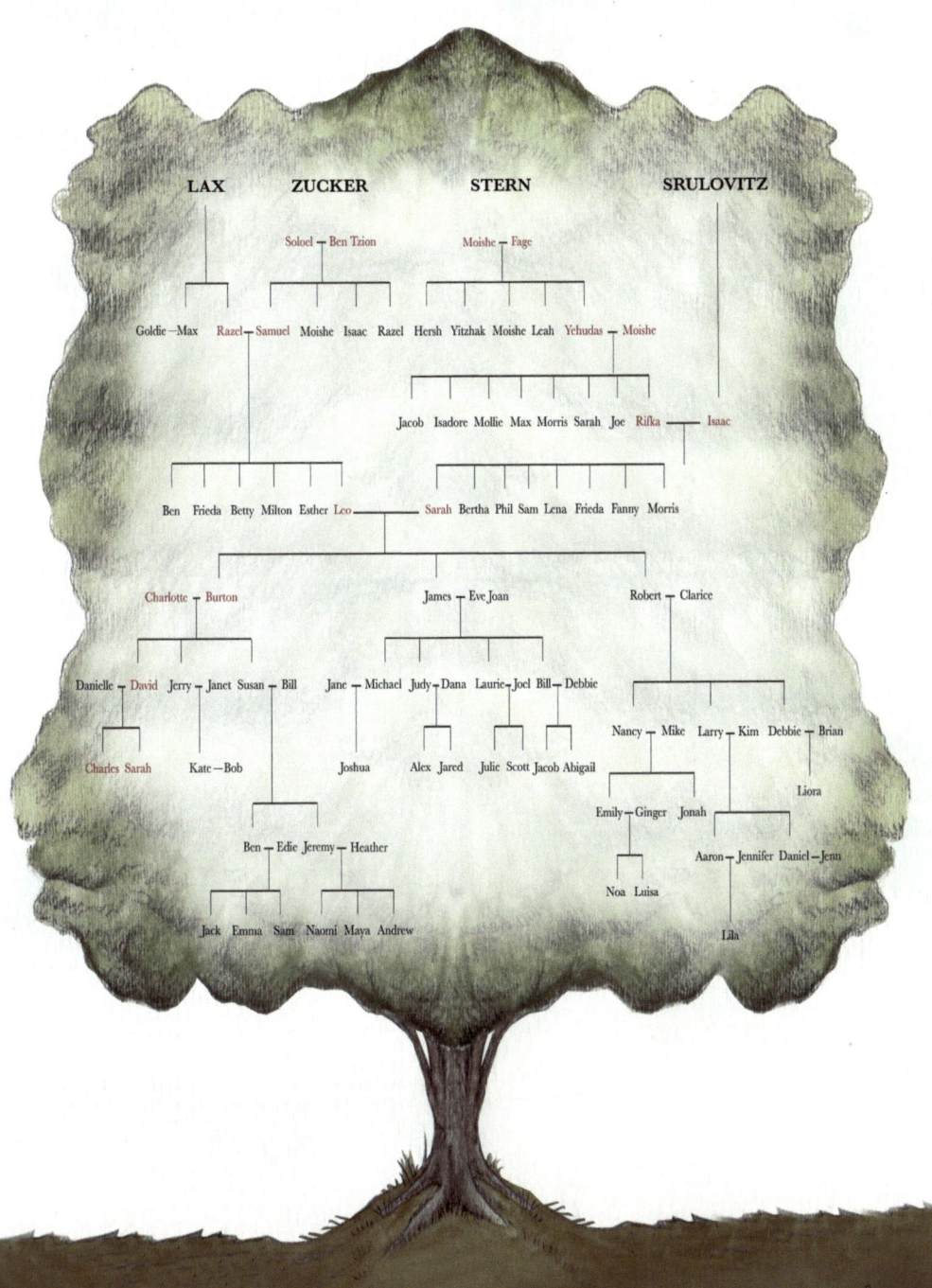

www.ingramcontent.com/pod-product-compliance
Lightning Source LLC
Chambersburg PA
CBHW041809160426
43209CB00028B/1901/J